BE Still

JILL LOWRY

ISBN-13: 978-0-578-79596-6

Be Still

Cover & Scripture Images Designed by Kerry Prater.
Interior Design by Katharine E. Hamilton

Scripture quotations are from the ESV® Bible (The
Holy Bible, English Standard Version®), copyright ©
2001 by Crossway, a publishing ministry of Good
News Publishers. Used by permission. All rights
reserved.

DEDICATION

This book is dedicated to the special people that God has placed in my life. As I am writing this, I am praising God for each of you. Thank you for encouraging me and loving me. I love you with all my heart!

INTRODUCTION

Do you believe that with God all things are possible? This wonderful promise is found in Matthew 19:26. God has many promises for you found in the pages of the Bible. He is waiting for you to "be still" and spend one-on-one time with Him each day as He speaks to your heart and encourages your soul with His promises of hope.

"Be Still" is a devotional that starts with a question derived from one scripture for each day of the year. Ponder the question, read the devotional, and pray the prayer at the end. Each day you will be in the Word of God as you read the highlighted scripture of promise from the Bible italicized for you. Focus on the promise, then pray the closing prayer that will strengthen your faith and enrich your soul.

This devotional combines scripture and prayer so you can spend one-on-one time with God by meditating on one scripture and then praying that scripture over your life. As you read His Words to you and pray to Him, your relationship will grow stronger and your faith will grow deeper. Put your finger on the promise, meditate on it, and pray the promise from your heart over your life and see how God will change you!

Psalm 119:10-16

"With my whole heart I seek you; let me not wander from your commandments!
I have stored up your word in my heart, that I might not sin against you.
Blessed are you, O LORD; teach me your statutes!
With my lips I declare all the rules of your mouth.
In the way of your testimonies I delight as much as in all riches.
I will mediate on your precepts and fix my eyes on your ways.
I will delight in your statutes; I will not forget your word."

Be still
AND KNOW
THAT
I am God.

PSALM 46:10

January 1

Are You Believing in the Impossible?

We all face situations that seem impossible. In these times, we must choose whether to press forward with faith or give up without hope. Some abandon everything when life gets tough. Others forge ahead faithfully, trusting God to work all things out. The ones who press on with God, who is always faithful, will see God show up immeasurably in their lives. For nothing is impossible with God! Greater things are possible when we take Him with us in all circumstances! With God in the center, impossibilities will be possible!

Dear Lord,

Thank You for making my impossible possible! I am trusting You. As I pray, I feel Your joy come alive inside me. Instead of focusing on problems, I am basking in the peace of Your love and grace. You hear my prayers, and You will answer in Your will and timing. While I wait for your response, I will trust You. For nothing is impossible with You! *"With man this is impossible, but with God all things are possible,"* Matthew 19:26.

In Jesus' Name, Amen

January 2

Are You Searching for Hope?

Are you worried about something so big that you cannot face it alone? Have you lost your hope? Hope is just around the corner when you call upon your Lord, your *living* hope, who is waiting to meet you right where you are! He is your HOPE — "Healer of Problems Eternally!"

We are surrounded by bad news today. As we focus on the news we hear and the problems we face, we feel hopeless and burdened. But with all the chaos and confusion, there is still hope! Our hope rests in a *living*, loving God who promises to never leave or abandon us. He will answer us even in our most challenging and desperate moments.

Dear Lord,

A new hope has come alive in me, and my heart is free from worry and fear as I draw closer to You. For I know when I need you most, You will answer as in Jeremiah 33:3, *"Call to me and I will answer you, and will tell you great and hidden things that you have not known."* You are my Healer of problems eternally!

In Jesus' Name, Amen

January 3

What are God's Plans for You?

There are many ways we can go, but only one way that leads to life. The way to life is through Jesus. You tell us that You are the way, the truth, and the life. Through You, is the only way we can have a relationship with the Father. All other paths lead to death. To know our plan, we must first have a close relationship to Jesus and let Him live inside us. We can hear His voice as we listen to the Holy Spirit and let go of our own will. Asking for guidance is the first step to knowing our plan.

Dear Lord,

I know You have plans for me, Lord. In you, there is great hope as my future rests in You. How can I know this plan? What is the plan You have for me? I thought I knew, but now I am unsure if it is Your plan for me or only what I want. I have found truth in Jeremiah 29:11, *"For I know the plans I have for you, declares the Lord, plans for wholeness and not for evil, to give you a future and a hope."* I pray I will trust you and keep in step with Your Word, Lord Jesus.

In Jesus' Name, Amen

January 4

Are You Looking for the Truth?

No one wants to live with lies and false promises that leave us hopeless. We know that we can be misled by what we hear and read if we do not know the truth. But how can we know *this* truth? Is it possible to discern what is false and what is true in this world where we live today? The truth is found in the Word of the Lord, which remains forever. All else will fade away. There is good news from our Lord which can be found as we seek His guidance in our lives in the pages of His Word.

Dear Lord,

I am seeking to live in the truth so that I can know how You want me to live day by day. In 1 Peter 1:24-25, I read that, *"All the flesh is like grass and all its glory like the flower of grass. The grass withers and the flower falls, but the word of the Lord remains forever."* I pray today that I will be guided by Your truth so You can set me free!

In Jesus' Name, Amen

January 5

How Can You Be Restored?

There are times in our life when we look around and realize we are missing something we once had present in us. We are restless and need restoration. We might look back to a time in our life where we felt peace and want to be back to that place. There was something different then and it is not present in us today. Was our life full of hope because we followed the Lord and let Him live in us? Were we fulfilled because our relationship to our Lord was alive and real in our lives? If it seems like the world has pulled you away from the arms of perfect peace and gentle love of your Lord, let Him restore you to Himself. He has been praying for you to return to His arms of grace.

Dear Lord,

I know that You will restore me as I pray for restoration as found in Lamentations 5:21, *"Restore us to yourself, O LORD, that we may be restored!"* I need You, Lord, to rescue me and give me rest. I want to come back to You! Restore me to Yourself!

In Jesus' Name, Amen

January 6

Are You Worried and Feeling Anxious Today?

There are countless things happening in our lives that can leave us worried and anxious. We become heavily burdened by these when we let them rule and control us. We are held captive by our own anxieties, especially when our mind is heavy with concerns and worries that flood our heart. God has come to take *all* these burdens from you. His arms are wide open to receive *everything* that you need to cast over to Him. As you cling to the Lord, you will find that *all* of your heart and your mind will finally be at peace. He is your *All* in *All*!

Dear Lord,

You will take over *everything* for me, so I can let go. In your Word, you say in 1 Peter 5:7 that I need to be *"casting all your anxieties on him, because he cares for you."* I admit that I have not been casting *all* of them to You. It is time for me to let go and let You take *all*, so that I can let You transform *all* of me!

In Jesus' Name, Amen

January 7

Do You Need to Be Forgiven?

You are not alone in your struggle. The Lord sees your challenge and wants you to come to Him with a humble heart so that He can wipe away every tear and fear. The hurtful things you said do not isolate you from the Lord. He is not angry with you. He has already forgiven you when you made Him the Lord of your life. He wants you to return to Him, so that He can make you whole again. The way to forgiveness is through our Lord Jesus Christ who is gracious and merciful to you!

Dear Lord,

Help me to see the areas in my life where I need to be made whole. Forgive me for the things I have done that are not pleasing to You. I want to obey your Word, so that You can heal my wounds. Your Word has come to life for me as I read Joel 2:13 and let this treasure comfort my soul, "*Return to the LORD your God, for he is gracious and merciful, slow to anger, and abounding in steadfast love.*" Your love and forgiveness have healed my soul and made me whole!

In Jesus' Name, Amen

January 8

Do You Need to Grow in Grace?

In this life, we will encounter those who hurt or offend us. We may be insulted or slandered unfairly. Our pride can get the best of us if we refuse to humble our hearts and offer grace to the offender. It is not easy to forgive, but the Lord knows that it is a sacrifice of love that must be made in order to set us free. He was the example of grace upon grace by bearing the cost and burden of our sins on the cross. He gave up His life in order that we may be free and forgiven by His grace! As we give grace, our life will be transformed, and as we forgive, we will be set free from our offenses and find new joy as the forgiver!

Dear Lord,

I am holding onto multiple offenses from my past, and it is time that I let go of them and forgive the offender. You want me to forgive, as you have forgiven me, by giving grace that flows from a humble heart. Your Word offers hope as I read in 2 Peter 3:18, *"But grow in the grace and knowledge of our Lord and Savior Jesus Christ."*

In Jesus' Name, Amen

January 9

Have You Lost Sight of Your Hope?

Are you struggling to see the light? Is the darkness of the world blinding you to the truth of the hope that God has for you? This world has darkness that does not come from God. When you set your mind on these worldly things, your hope vanishes into the darkness. Set your eyes on Jesus Christ who will surround you with the light of His love and mercy. There is greater hope ahead for those who live in the light of Christ!

Dear Lord,

I want to live in the light of Your hope! Help me shift my focus to You, Lord. My mind has been preoccupied with the problems of this world. Forgive me for worrying about my problems and not focusing on You. I see the light when I step out of the dark and into the path of Your marvelous light! You remind me in 1 John 1:5, *"God is light, and in him is no darkness at all."* I will live each moment in Your light. My hope grows and my light shines for all to see that the hope in me comes from You, my Lord!

In Jesus' Name, Amen

January 10

Are You Feeling Insecure?

There are times when we are running well and getting a lot accomplished in our own effort and control. We may be on "top of the world" and feeling great, and then, something happens, and we lose our strength and our hope. It can be sudden or gradual, but we finally start giving up. All the running on our own has worn us out. We feel alone as we have been striving to be the best by ourselves. Someone we depended on has let us down, and we find ourselves feeling insecure once again. Alone, insecure, and weak is not what God wants for us. God wants us to look to Him for strength so He can lift us up to higher ground!

Dear Lord,

I have found myself trying too hard to please people rather than please You, my audience of one. I am worn out and weary from trying to do it on my own. As I read Habakkuk 3:19, *"God, the Lord, is my strength; he makes my feet like the deer's; he makes me tread on my high places,"* I am encouraged to get my strength for the home stretch from You, Lord!

In Jesus' Name, Amen

January 11

Are You Reaching for Love?

As we reach out to others with kindness, we are showing our love for them. People need to see our love in our actions and deeds and not just hear us "talk the talk." As we walk in love that flows from a giving heart, people feel loved. As many will confirm, most people do not remember what we say, but they remember how we make them feel. As we reach out to give our love, we show the love of Jesus. What the world needs now, is *love, sweet love*!

Dear Lord,

Thank You for the love You give to me. You gave me the greatest love when You sacrificed all for me. I know I am loved as You reached out to me through Your ultimate act of love. The truth of Your love can be found at the foot of the cross. You ask me to love others as Your word teaches in 1 John 3:18, "*Little children, let us not love in word or talk but in deed and in truth.*" The love of Jesus is the key that opens the heart all the time!

In Jesus' Name, Amen

January 12

Do You Need Help for the
Battle You are Facing?

Are you in a battle right now? Have you lost your faith because you are looking at the problem and it seems impossible? Nothing is impossible and no problem is too big for your God! Believe that He will help you and lift you up out of the pit. Take His hand, and He will rescue you. Believe that His shield will protect you and His gentle touch of love will give you peace and comfort. Look up child, and let the Lord lift up your head!

Dear Lord,

I am in need of Your powerful, loving touch upon my life in these struggles I am facing. My heart is heavy with burdens upon me and with those I see for others around me. It seems like I hear another story each day that breaks my heart even further. You say to look to You for hope and call upon You for help as I read in, Psalm 3:3, *"But you, O LORD, are a shield about me, my glory, and the lifter of my head."* I am comforted by this truth as I cling to You, my shield, my glory, and the lifter of my head!

In Jesus' Name, Amen

January 13

How Long Until Your Prayers are Answered?

We do not like to wait. We want quick answers to our questions and solutions to our problems. Our patience is tested when we must simply wait. The waiting can be the hardest part of our struggle and the most frustrating part of the challenge. We can have this same attitude when we pray. As we pray, we hope for immediate answers in the time frame we ask. It is true that He hears our prayers the second we pray. But what about the timing? How long must we wait? We wait for his perfect timing and will.

Dear Lord,

Psalm 13:1 begins with the words, *"How long, O Lord?"* I have the same question as well. I am wondering how long I must wait. But I will wait upon You, my Lord. My heart is full of promise and hope because I know that whatever the answers might be, You are here right beside me, steadfastly loving me. The answers will come in Your perfect timing. You will answer as I keep praying!

In Jesus' Name, Amen

January 14

What Are You Seeking?

We are all seeking something. We have needs deep down in our souls. We have dreams and hopes for our future. We set goals to achieve success in our lives. We want to find happiness, so we work harder to accomplish things that we think will bring fulfillment. We want to be loved, so we seek love from people in our lives. We need, so we seek. Jesus asks us *what* we are seeking, because He wants us to seek Him first. He yearns to fill our hearts with His love. We were created with the need to be loved. He knows that our hearts are empty without love, so He invites us to seek Him with all our hearts so that He can fill us with His eternal love!

Dear Lord,

As I read Your question in John 1:38, *"What are you seeking?"* I will be still and ponder this for myself. As I pray, it is clear that all I need can be found in You. You are the way, the truth, and the life. You will never leave me. When I seek You, I will find You. I am seeking You, Jesus!

In Jesus' Name, Amen

January 15

Do You Hear the Gentle Whisper?

Do you hear the gentle whisper of the Spirit of God calling you? Did you know that the Father has given you a gift that you can have if you choose? This gift is the Holy Spirit who will be with you forever. He will guide you into all truth and lead you to greater love if you let Him. Life in the Spirit brings real peace, hope, and joy that can never be taken away. The Holy Spirit is alive in you when you let go. This same power that raised Jesus from the dead lives in you!

Dear Lord,

I am listening to the still voice of Your beautiful Spirit stirring inside of me. You have gently whispered, and I will listen to You. I know that Jesus wanted to give me a Helper, as I read in John 14:16, *"And I will ask the Father, and he will give you another Helper, to be with you forever."* This Helper is the Holy Spirit who has given me new life and direction as I choose to live in the Spirit. Holy Spirit, You are welcome in my life! I am letting Your whisper of love into my heart for eternity!

In Jesus' Name, Amen

January 16

Do You Have Sorrow Now?

We have all experienced sorrow in this world. When someone we love passes from this earth, we feel the deepest sorrow, loss, and loneliness. We miss these loved ones so much and wish we could see them again. The good news is that we have been given hope through Jesus that we will see our loved ones again in Heaven one day! The friends of Jesus knew these feelings well as He departed from this earth to be with the Father. He knew they would be filled with sorrow and pain, so He left them with hope in the person of the Holy Spirit who would live inside them and give them eternal joy!

Dear Lord,

You know my sorrow and pain well, Lord. You see inside my heart like no one else can. You have given me complete joy, even in the shadow of pain, because I have invited You to live in my heart. I believe Your Word in John 16:22, *"So also you have sorrow now, but I will see you again and your hearts will rejoice, and no one will take your joy from you."*

In Jesus' Name, Amen

January 17

Why Must You Wait?

Are you waiting for answers? The Lord wants you to wait upon Him. Let Him build you up with His love and encouragement instead of despair and discouragement as you are awaiting answers. He will strengthen you to endure whatever you are facing. He will preserve you from trouble as you keep close to Him. Have you made the choice to follow Him with all integrity and uprightness even when you are tempted? When the temptations come, He will give you a way out. Wait upon the Lord by trusting His plan. All things will work out for good for those who love the Lord and are called according to His purpose. Stay the course with all integrity and uprightness, for your answers are coming!

Dear Lord,

As I pray, I know that I must wait upon You and Your will to be done. Psalm 25:21 gives me direction as I read, "*May integrity and uprightness preserve me, for I wait for you.*" I will grow in grace and knowledge as Your plan unfolds for me just at the right time. My waiting will build my integrity and uprightness as I look to You, my anchor of hope!

In Jesus' Name, Amen

January 18

Are You Struggling with Sin?

Have you lost your hope because your sins have weighed you down? Is your face turned to sin and your back to God? Turn around and seek the face of God! The Lord has forgiven you and wants to set you free. He has been waiting for you to open your heart to his invitation. The grace of the Lord is a free gift of God for you to receive as you invite His Son, Jesus, into your heart. Say *yes* to the hope of Heaven found in Jesus, the power of Holy Spirit, and the grace-filled love of God. You *will* be set free!

Dear Lord,

The struggle with sin is real. You know what I will face each day, so You have given me Your Word and Your Spirit to encourage me to hold fast to You. Your powerful presence has given me courage to say no to the flesh and yes to the Spirit. In Psalm 27:8, *"You have said, 'Seek my face.' My heart says to you, 'Your face, Lord, do I seek.'"* As I seek Your face, my heart will be open to the light of Your love and grace.

In Jesus' Name, Amen

January 19

Are You Hoping to See Unity Among All?

Are you hoping to see unity among all people? Is peace possible where there is so much division? Yes, all things are possible with God! Unity is possible for all who believe in the God of the impossible. You can see unity as you come together with an open heart to live in harmony. Instead of complaining, how about looking for the good in every situation? Start the day with positive thinking instead of allowing negative thoughts to enter your mind and come out of your mouth. Feel the love of God warm your heart as you allow His love to embrace you. Give thanks for the people who have fought for your freedom and hold on to the promise of unity through Christ!

Dear Lord,

My prayer is to see unity where there is division. In Acts 2:44, Your word reads,"*And all who believed were together and had all things in common.*" Let us all come together and believe that we can set aside our self-serving agenda and use our gifts and talents to serve You! United we will stand but divided we will fall!

In Jesus' Name, Amen

January 20

Are You Looking for Direction?

Are you needing help and guidance with something today? Is your heart heavy with decisions weighing you down and you do not know where to turn? Do you need a guiding hand to direct you as you go? There is hope for you! God has promised to guide you in the right direction if you will invite Him into your life and ask Him to direct your steps. His Word is clear in Psalm 32:8, *"I will instruct you and teach you in the way you should go."* How comforting it is to know this truth found in the Lord! Let Him lead you on the right path that leads to everlasting life!

Dear Lord,

Thank you for leading me on the right path. I will get lost without Your guiding light. I need You every day to direct each thought, word, and action that I take. It is so good to be close to You, my Lord. Thank You for instructing me in the truth as I read Your Word. Give me this day my daily bread, so I can grow closer to Your love and direction for my life!

In Jesus' Name, Amen

January 21

Have You Praised God Today?

We pray to our Lord and He hears every single prayer we pray. It is amazing to know He listens to every word. He sees inside our hearts and knows our thoughts. As we pray, He loves to hear us praise Him with thankful hearts. As we are waiting for answers, our faith grows as we lift our prayers and praises before Him. While we sit in the "waiting room," let us praise our mighty God who knows everything about us and has the best plans for us! He yearns to hear our hearts! In Psalm 34:3, we read these encouraging words, *"Oh magnify the LORD with me, and let us exalt his name together!"*

Dear Lord,

I praise you today for being the Lord of my heart! You have given me buckets of hope and joy that have filled me up. I am walking with a song of praise in my heart, even as I wait for Your plan to unfold for me. I am thankful to You and will magnify Your glorious name. My cup overflows with gratitude and praise!

In Jesus' Name, Amen

January 22

Are You Waiting for God to Reveal Wisdom to You?

We all have plans for our lives and hope to make wise choices. We plan our future and make goals for what we want to achieve each day. Our plans can be good, but when we add God to our lives, commit our way to Him and trust Him, He will give us great wisdom as He reveals His plans for us in His perfect timing. As we allow God to go before us, He will open the door to many blessings of wisdom. His truth brings hope as it says in Psalm 37:5, *"Commit your way to the Lord; trust in him, and he will act."*

Dear Lord,

I am listening with my heart as I commit my way to You. I will trust You and lean not on my own understanding. In all my ways I will search for Your wisdom by staying close to You and Your words of truth. As I do, You will direct my path. Thank you for bringing me peace, as I wait upon You to impart Your wisdom! I will wait upon You so that I can fly with the power of Your Spirit!

In Jesus' Name, Amen

January 23

Are You Ready to Give Up?

Are you ready to quit? Is the work you are doing making you weary? Have you just about given up because you do not have the strength or will to press on? The Lord knows your heart and hears your cries for help. In Psalm 40:1, there are words of encouragement just for you. *"I waited patiently for the LORD; He inclined to me and heard my cry."* Wait upon the Lord as you press into His Word and Spirit. He is waiting for you to ask for help, so that He can help you finish strong as you press on with the power and presence of Jesus Christ!

Dear Lord,

I need Your help to press on with the work You have given me. I will wait patiently upon You as I work each day. You are my strength when I am weak and my anchor of hope when I feel like giving up. I know that if I stay the course and work with You, I can keep going strong. If I go alone I will eventually wear out. Thank You for lifting me up and giving me Your endurance for this race.

In Jesus' Name, Amen

January 24

Is Hope Possible Through Your Suffering?

Are you struggling with pain? Is your suffering so real that you are not sure if you can make it any longer? Are you so hurt that you have lost your hope? Turn from the pain and seek the mighty hand of God to restore you! Surrender all your hurt for His fresh hope and cling to His promise in Romans 5:3-4, "We *rejoice in our sufferings, knowing that suffering produces endurance, and endurance produces character, and character produces hope.*" The sufferings you are experiencing will produce endurance and character that will help you grow fresh faith which leads to hope in Jesus Christ. Hope is possible!

Dear Lord,

Struggles are real in this life. Only You, without sin, know what it is like to suffer death on the cross for the sins of all. Jesus, You defeated death which has given all of us new life! As I struggle, I will remember what You did for me and cling to the hope that is found in You. Thank You for touching my heart with Your redeeming love and renewed hope.

In Jesus' Name, Amen

January 25

Is Your Heart Heavy with Troubles?

We all have times of trouble and heartache. We will have moments where our strength is gone, and our hearts are filled with sadness. But we still have good news in these times. We can let our hearts be filled with praise, because when we face troubled times, we have a rescuer and a rock of hope, Jesus Christ! Our Lord does not want our hearts to be troubled but wants us to find our refuge and strength in Him! He will help us overcome and persevere! Soak up His words of comfort in Psalm 46:1, "*God is our refuge and strength, a vey present help in trouble.*" Turn to God for help! He will comfort you with His love and help you overcome your sadness.

Dear Lord,

I am praising You today for giving me strength and fullness of joy! You are my rock of refuge and shield of protection. Thank You for being a present help to me in times where my heart is troubled. Only You can take away all my sadness and wipe away my tears with songs of thanksgiving and praise! I praise Your Holy name with a Hallelujah!

In Jesus' Name, Amen

January 26

Are You Believing that All Will Work Out for Good?

Are you believing that all things will work out for good? Have you seen God work in mighty ways in your life? Are you ready to see God move in your heart and soul? Trust in the Lord to work all things out for you. Trust and believe the promise in Romans 8:28, "*And we know that for those who love God all things work together for good, for those who are called according to his purpose.*" Believe that you will see God working all things out for good!

Dear Lord,

Thank You for being present in my life. Even when I do not understand, You are working all things out for good. Your blessings are overwhelming and overpowering in the best way. I am blessed beyond measure just to know You as my Lord and Savior! I am thankful for Your bountiful blessings. Help me to let go and let you work all things out for me in Your timing. I know Your plan is perfect for me. I am giving thanks today with a grateful heart!

In Jesus' Name, Amen

January 27

Are You Wanting to be Set Free?

Are you looking to be set free from sin? Do you feel lost or know someone else that is struggling to be set free? Romans 10:9 guarantees, *"If you confess with your mouth that Jesus is Lord and believe in your heart that God raised him from the dead, you will be saved."* Salvation is possible for everyone who believes! This is the good news that changes everyone and everything! Your Savior, Jesus Christ, is waiting for you! Let Jesus touch your heart with His enduring grace and everlasting life, and you will be set free!

Dear Lord,

Thank You for this good news of salvation that is for all who believe! I once was lost before I confessed and believed in You as my Savior. I know what it is like to struggle and live without Your saving grace and eternal life. But now I see You, Lord! You have found me and pulled me out of the pit of sin into your arms of love and forgiveness! Your Spirit has come alive inside of me to direct and guide my thoughts and actions. I am set free in You, my Savior!

In Jesus' Name, Amen

January 28

How Can We Live with More Hope When Negativity Surrounds Us?

We hear the bad news that surrounds us, and our hearts become burdened. We want to find hope, but in all the negativity around us, we struggle. It is hard to find peace in a world where the negative news is at the forefront. We can get so involved with the world, that our minds become conformed to this world. When we take our focus off Jesus, our minds can shift to these other matters. But there is hope when we let Jesus transform and renew our minds. *"Do not be conformed to this world, but be transformed by the renewal of your mind."* Romans 12:2

Dear Lord,

I am seeking more of You so that I can have more hope in this world where peace does not reign. When I turn my focus to You, my mind becomes more centered on the peace that you bring. I am content when I let You work inside of me. You are the answer to my restless and burdened heart! I will let you transform me!

In Jesus' Name, Amen

January 29

Are You Needing More Peace?

Are you in need of more peace in your life because your heart is heavy with troubles and your mind restless with worries? Turn back to your peacemaker, the Lord, Jesus Christ, who will give you lasting, perfect peace! He is waiting for you to be filled with His peace. Pursue Him, and you will find the peace that you have lost. As you pursue the peace of Christ, others around you will experience peace as well. *"So then let us pursue what makes for peace and for mutual upbuilding,"* Romans 14:19.

Dear Lord,

I will pursue You to find my peace. I am ready to experience eternal, perfect peace that only You can give me. As I open my heart to the peace of Christ and close it to the worry of the world, I feel a renewed peace cover my heart, body, mind, and soul. It is good to feel Your peace, Lord! I need You every moment of my life as I hear and see problems all around me. Peace is the presence of You in my life, not the absence of problems! I will pursue You, my Prince of Peace!

In Jesus' Name, Amen

January 30

What is Distracting You?

Is your mind filled with distractions that heavily weigh you down? Are you ready to see a shift in your heart by shedding negative thoughts and turning them into more positive thinking? Do you hope that you can find more positivity, but need your mind to be clear of all the clutter? Let Jesus renew your mind by shifting your attention to Him. He is calling you to a deeper relationship with Him by allowing Him to work inside your heart. He is calling you to pray, read His Word, and surround yourself with like-minded people to encourage you. He wants you to think about things worthy of praise, even in a world of distractions.

Dear Lord,

I know You are the answer. I trust You more than anything or anyone else. I am putting my faith in You, so You will renew my mind and restore my hope. *"Finally, brothers, whatever is true, whatever is honorable, whatever is just, whatever is pure, whatever is lovely, whatever is commendable, if there is any excellence, if there is anything worthy of praise, think about these things,"* Philippians 4:8.

In Jesus' Name, Amen

January 31

Have You Found Your Joy in Jesus?

Are you overwhelmed by your problems and tasks at hand? Do you feel like you are carrying so much worry that you have lost your joy? Do you need a fresh filling of the Spirit? Look to the Lord Jesus Christ for all your needs. Pray that you will focus on Jesus and His great love for you. Ask Him to restore your joy as you celebrate the good news of His birth all year long! *"For unto you is born this day in the city of David a Savior, who is Christ the Lord." Luke 2:11* Let this good news settle in your heart and you will discover an everlasting joy!

Dear Lord,

I am rejoicing again for the good news of great joy that is found in my Savior, the Lord Jesus Christ! Thank You for this miracle birth of a Savior who loves me! The problems I face are real, but You are greater than anything I will ever encounter! I am magnifying You with all that is in me. I bask in Your glory with a joyful heart!

In Jesus' Name, Amen

Monthly Reflections

As you pray and lean on the Lord's promises, write what the Lord has revealed to you for this month.

DELIGHT YOURSELF
in the Lord,
AND HE WILL GIVE
you the desires
of your heart.
PSALM 37:4

February 1

Will Your Choices Today Honor the Lord?

We all have times where we face temptations. As we make decisions each day, we are one choice away from honor. As we choose the Lord our God and honor Him, He is well pleased. When we struggle, He promises to give us strength to choose the right way and give us the courage to stand up for what *is* right. As we worship Him, He gives us strength to say no to the temptations and yes to righteous and holiness. *"So then, brothers, stand firm and hold to the traditions that you were taught by us, either by our spoken word or by our letter,"* 2 Thessalonians 2:15.

Dear Lord,

Today, I pray that as I clothe myself in Your love and grace, that I can make decisions that will honor You. I will say *no* to self and *yes* to You, my Lord, who sacrificed all for me! Thank You for loving me and helping me be the best I can be for You. As I grow closer to Your heartbeat, I will grow love, joy, peace, patience, kindness, goodness, faithfulness, gentleness, and self-control.

In Jesus' Name, Amen

February 2

Do You Want to be Healed?

We all have the need to be healed. We are all under construction. None of us are perfect and can say we do not need healing. Healing is good and exactly what our Lord can do for us when we ask Him. He has the power to heal us. He is waiting for us to ask for Him to heal us. Nothing is impossible with God! Believe that healing is possible and keep praying for that miracle. As we ask for healing, we must remind ourselves that the Lord heals in His timing and for His glory. Keep praying and draw closer to the Lord for your healing.

Dear Lord,

I am so thankful for Your healing power! I want to be healed where You know I need it most. As I draw closer to You, my struggles disappear, and my pains subside. *"O LORD my God, I cried to you for help, and you have healed me."* Psalm 30:2. I believe in Your healing for me, and I receive all You have for me! Let it be, Lord Jesus!

In Jesus' Name, Amen

February 3

Have You Continued to Pray for What is on Your Heart?

Are you seeking peace and direction? Do you want to grow closer to your Lord? Take time to pray like Jesus did. Go to a place where you can get away from distractions, be by yourself, and where you can share your heart in prayer. Spend time with God. Let Jesus be your example as He made time to pray as Luke 6:12 reads, *"In these days, he went out to the mountain to pray, and all night he continued in prayer to God."* Jesus continued to pray. Have you continued your prayers even when you have not seen an answer? Keep faithfully pouring out your heart as you pray to a loving God who opens the heavens as you pray!

Dear Lord,

Thank you for this power of prayer. I have grown closer to You as my prayer life has continued to deepen. I love knowing that You hear every prayer that I pray. I will continue to pray, so that I can keep hearing Your voice! Speak to me. I am listening as I sit at your feet!

In Jesus' Name, Amen

February 4

Whose Voice are You Listening to?

There are many voices all around us trying to get our attention. We live in a world where everyone wants to be right and has an opinion. If we are not careful, we can be pulled in the direction of the voice that is the loudest instead of the voice of truth. It is easy to hear the booming voices around us when we let our ears hear and focus on these voices instead of the still small voice of the Spirit of God inside of us. Let us listen with ears to hear our Lord God! In Luke 8:8 He says, "*He who has ears to hear, let him hear.*"

Dear Lord,

Help me to tune out the voices that are not what You want me to hear and help me tune into Your voice. I know that Your plan is best, so I will listen to what You are speaking to me. My ears are open to hear Your voice of truth. As I hear Your voice, I will trust and obey. I am so thankful I have ears to hear You, my Lord! My ears are open to hear and act as You direct me in love!

In Jesus' Name, Amen

February 5

Are You Walking by Faith?

Have you decided to trust the Lord with all your heart and lean on His faithfulness? Are you looking for help to navigate the decisions facing you? Do you need more faith? Keep believing and trusting the Lord with all your heart even when you cannot see all the details. He is with you every step of the way as He directs all your steps. Lean on the Lord and let Him guide you by His faithfulness. He will show you the way and save you! Let faith come alive inside of you! *"And he said to the woman, "Your faith has saved you; go in peace,"* Luke 7:50.

Dear Lord,

I know I am saved by faith. I am sure of what I hope for and will let my faith in You be my eyes. I have said yes to faith and have let Your peace cover every part of me. It is so good to be led by faith as I live with Your saving grace. Peace has settled over me as I let You lead me. Thank You for Your peace that passes understanding. I can confidently walk by faith!

In Jesus' Name, Amen

February 6

Have You Praised God for His Majesty?

God has created all things in His majesty. He has made everything beautiful and wonderful for all to see! He makes beauty from ashes and brings hope in the darkness. His glory shines in all that He creates for us to experience. The wonderment of His power glows brightly in all His creation. As His light brightens the darkness, we can see miracles come alive for us. The miracle He has for us begins in the renewal of our heart as we draw closer to His love. In Luke 9:43, many praised God for His glory and *"All were astonished at the majesty of God."* When is the last time you were astonished by the majesty of God? He wants you to see His glory and come closer to His love today!

Dear Lord,

Thank You for Your majesty and glory! I am overwhelmed by Your powerful presence and it is so good to be able to see Your hand in all things. As I come closer to Your love, my heart glows with Your Holy Fire inside of me! I will praise You, my Lord, for Your majesty!

In Jesus' Name, Amen

February 7

What do Your Eyes See?

We have been created by God to have eyes to see. God has given us eyes to see His wonder and beauty. He has given us eyes to see people with His eyes of grace. God has blessed us with the miracle of vision to be able to see all. As we give God praise for His many blessings, let us not forget to thank Him for our vision. As we look into the eyes of those we love, we see our blessings given to us by God! As we see the sparkle of light shine in the eyes of our friends, we see Jesus! As we look at the beauty of God's creations, we see His glory and majesty! His miracles are all around us when we open our eyes to see! *"Blessed are the eyes that see what you see!"* Luke 10:23

Dear Lord,

I will look through my spiritual eyes to see what You want me to see. I will keep looking for opportunities to bless others for Your glory. As I keep my eyes wide open, I will also keep an open heart. Thank you for expanding my vision and territory to see outside of me.

In Jesus' Name, Amen

February 8

Are You Obeying the Word of God?

God has given us His Word to hear and keep close to our hearts for our good. He never leads us down the wrong path when we listen and obey. His instruction manual for life is found in the pages of the Holy Bible. Each verse gives us direction and answers to questions for us today. God will guide us down the right path when we obey the truth found in His Word. Receive your blessings from the Lord of everlasting love! *"Blessed rather are those who hear the word of God and keep it!" Luke 11:28.*

Dear Lord,

I want to keep listening to You and obeying Your Word of truth. Help me to stay connected to You by applying the pages of Your Word to my life! I want to be closer to You, and that starts with my choice to trust and obey You each step of the way. As I obey, I find the power of Your Word and the Holy Spirit coming alive inside of me! It is through my obedience that my faith grows! I am praising You for the abundant blessings that flow from hearing Your Word and keeping it!

In Jesus' Name, Amen

February 9

Which Door are You Seeking to Enter?

We all have choices about the direction we will go. There are multiple doors to choose from, but only one door that leads to life. The narrow path of promise can only be found when we follow Jesus Christ and open *His* door. He leads us on the straight and narrow path that is beautiful and filled with peace and freedom. When we venture off this path, we get lost and miss our blessings found on the road with Jesus. Step out in faith by getting back on the straight and narrow road of Jesus that will bring you home! He is waiting for you to get back on the path with Him! "*Strive to enter through the narrow door. For many, I tell you, will seek to enter and will not be able,*" Luke 13:24.

Dear Lord,

I see the light of Your love as I step into my destiny through Your door. My path is clearer when I trust You with all my heart and lean not on my own understanding. In all my ways I will acknowledge You, so that You will make my path straight on Your road.

In Jesus' Name, Amen

February 10

Have You Heard the Good News?

Have you heard the good news of Jesus Christ? Is Jesus Christ in the center of your life and foremost in your heart? Open your ears to listen to His love and let Him inside your heart. He wants to grow a garden of love in you as you come into a deeper relationship with Him. He yearns for you to listen to His voice calling you closer. Have you drifted away? Come back home to the Lord who speaks truth to you and will restore you. He is speaking to you out of love. Be still and listen with your heart! In Luke 14:35, the Lord directs you as He speaks, *"He who has ears to hear, let him hear."*

Dear Lord,

I am listening to Your voice as I am still before you. It is good to be close to You as I sit at Your feet and pray from my heart. I know You hear each prayer and know each thought. I am blessed to know You personally and intimately as my Lord and Savior! You have forgiven me because You love me! I am graced and humbled to be Your child created with ears to hear You!

In Jesus' Name, Amen

BE STILL

February 11

Have You Asked God for Forgiveness?

Are you struggling with sin and need a way out? Is your heart aching for joy, but you do not know how to find it? Has your peace left you because you keep going back in your mind to your mistakes and regrets? Come as you are to Jesus. He is the answer to the emptiness you feel deep down in your soul. He will fill your heart with more joy and peace than you could possibly imagine as you confess your need for a Savior and trust Him with all of your heart! You are one step away from freedom and one choice away from honor. In Luke 15:10, Jesus declares, *"There is joy before the angels of God over one sinner who repents."* Keep drawing closer in your heart to Jesus and you *will* find the joy your heart desires! Hear the angels rejoicing!

Dear Lord,

You have forgiven me so that I can be free of the chains of sin that so easily entangle me. I pray that my choices will honor You. Thank You for the joy that You have so freely given me as I repent and believe that Your grace has saved me!

In Jesus' Name, Amen

February 12

Are You Staying Faithful?

Are you letting God work inside of you? Have you said *yes* to God and *no* to temptations that pull you away from His will for you? He will show you the way as you stay faithful! Keep letting Him take the wheel of your life so you can go in the best direction. When the Lord is your pilot, your faith will be your eyes. He is steering you to freedom and will take over for you. The temptations will cease as you let God take control. Stay close to the Lord, and you will stay faithful and righteous before Him! *"One who is faithful in a very little is also faithful in much, and one who is dishonest in a very little is also dishonest in much,"* Luke 16:10.

Dear Lord,

I want to stay faithful to You. I see You at work even in the little things! Your eyes see for me when I let You take control. You navigate my course when I give You the wheel. Even when I cannot see, You are there guiding me. Your angels are all around me protecting me! I feel Your presence in my life, and I am humbled and blessed!

In Jesus' Name, Amen

February 13

Has the Healing Power of God Touched You?

Are you struggling to see? Have you lost your hope in all the darkness around you? Let go of your troubles and come to the light of Christ by faith. Your faith will become your eyes to see as you keep going. Press on to glory and see what is in store for you, faithful one! His love lights the way for you, and you are touched by His healing when you step out in faith and believe! Let His healing touch you and make you whole as you step out in faith! As Luke 17:19 proclaims, *"Rise and go your way; your faith has made you well."*

Dear Lord,

I know that my faith in You will bring healing to my heart and soul as I grow closer to Your love. You have encouraged me to press on and finish strong. As I continue on this faith journey with You, I will grow stronger and experience total healing! My heart rejoices today as I magnify Your name!

In Jesus' Name, Amen

February 14

Do You Believe Your Impossible is Possible?

Nothing is impossible with God! He is the creator of all things and has the power over everything. He can do what seems impossible for man. Trust Him to work all things out in His timing and with His power. His glory shines forth even in the most difficult days when we trust Him with all our hearts. Keep believing for that miracle. Keep hoping for that promise to become reality. Keep praying for what seems impossible to be possible. All things are possible with our God! *"What is impossible with man is possible with God,"* Luke 18:27.

Dear Lord,

It is time for me to surrender all to You. I have been holding on to worry and things I cannot control. I have let my fear stop me from seeing the impossible become possible with You! Your promises will come to light for me as I stay faithful to You! Help me to stay the course with courage while living in Your peace! It is time to let go and let You work all things out for my good and for Your glory!

In Jesus' Name, Amen

February 15

Do You Feel the Peace of the Lord?

Are you wanting peace? Is your problem drawing you away from the peace you are seeking? Feel the light of God's love cover every part of you. If you believe in His son, Jesus Christ, as your personal Savior, His perfect peace is yours to have. It is time for you to come to the Lord God who will give you His peace. As you praise God from whom all blessings flow, you will discover His peaceful blessings. *"Blessed is the King who comes in the name of the Lord! Peace in heaven and glory in the highest!"* Luke 19:38.

Dear Lord,

I want Your perfect peace! I will let go of my worries and let Your peace surround me. Thank You for giving me this peace that will reign in me as I keep trusting You with my whole heart! It is so good to be loved by You, my Prince of Peace! Your peace reigns in me as I grow in Your grace and truth. I will let go of my problems and let You solve them with Your perfect peace!

In Jesus' Name, Amen

February 16

Are You Living to Please the Lord Who Loves You?

Are you ready to see the love of God come alive inside of you? Have you given Him your heart so that He can work in your life? Will you aim to please the Lord in all that you do so that you can live closer to His love? As you trust the Lord more each day, He will work inside of you to accomplish His will for you. His plan is always best. Trust Him completely. His faith will overshadow you so that your faith can grow. Let God rule over your heart and you will come alive! *"Now he is not God of the dead, but of the living, for all to live to him," Luke 20:38.*

Dear Lord,

As I let Your love reign inside of me, I can see Your hand upon me working all things out in Your will and Your way. It feels so good to let Your love come alive inside of me! Thank You for helping me to see Your love in a special way! I will trust and obey You even in the most difficult times.

In Jesus' Name, Amen

February 17

Have You Lost Your Strength And Endurance?

Life on this earth is a race. Some run through life savoring each moment and some sprint through life never noticing the beauty and blessings all around them. But how are we running our race? As we press on to the finish line and see the victory ahead of us, we must have strength and endurance to persevere. Only God can get us to the finish line so we can receive our reward. With Christ in our lives, our victory and reward are already secured. *"By your endurance you will gain your lives,"* Luke 21:19.

Dear Lord,

I want to savor all the blessings around me as I run my race. I will run with endurance so I can finish strong. I will not stop pressing on with You but will run my race with perseverance. You are my shield and my song as I run with steadfastness. I press on in the challenges and see them as possibilities to grow my faith and build my character. As I run with You, I see the light all around me, all the way to the finish line!

In Jesus' Name, Amen

February 18

Have You Prayed for Faith?

It is easy to give up when we do not yet see what we hoped for happening in our lives. If we live by only what we see, fear and worry set in and our faith can fail. Our faith will come alive if we live, by faith, for what we hope for instead of by worry and fear of what might happen without faith. Let us pray for our faith to grow and spread to others around us. When faith comes to our life, new life emerges within us. We will spring forward to new challenges when we let faith take over fear. Help our faith to grow as we pray! *"I have prayed for you that your faith may not fail. And when you have turned again, strengthen your brothers,"* Luke 22:32.

Dear Lord,

I want to keep walking faithfully with You one step at a time. As I pray, I will face each challenge as new opportunities to grow in faith. It is so good to know that I can walk by faith with You. Help me to take off fear and put on faith. I am praying that my faith will be bigger than my fear so I can clearly see You!

In Jesus' Name, Amen

February 19

Have You Laid Your Sins Down at the Cross?

Have you asked Jesus to forgive you? Are you believing God will wipe away every tear and fear? Ask Jesus to forgive you of your sins and believe that He died for those sins and will give you eternal life! Jesus has asked the Father for you to be forgiven. You will receive all you need when you come to the cross. He is waiting for you! Believe that Jesus loves you! The words spoken in Luke 23:34 bring us hope as Jesus speaks, *"Father, forgive them, for they know not what they do."* When you say *yes* to Jesus, you become a child of God, forgiven and free!

Dear Lord,

Thank You for forgiving me. I know that You love me so much that You have given Your Son, Jesus Christ as a sacrifice for my sins. I am thankful and blessed to have Jesus as my Savior! I will spread this message of hope found in You. I am grateful for this hope that is real. I am rejoicing in Your love and humbled by Your grace! My victory is in Jesus Christ!

In Jesus' Name, Amen

February 20

Do You Know the Present Peace of Christ?

Do you know the peace of Christ? Have you felt His joy deep in your soul? Is your heart full of hope that comes from the Lord? The Lord loves you and wants you to keep your faith. A life without faith is one that is dominated by doubt. Keep believing and hold tight to His perfect peace that is given to you. Luke 24:36 gives you a blessing of present peace from Jesus as He says, *"Peace to you!"* Christ the Lord has come to give you peace! Let His peace settle in your heart forever!

Dear Lord,

Thank You for the perfect peace that You have given me as I trust You. I have taken Your peace and have let it settle deep in my soul. Your peace is wonderful, and I am thankful You are my Lord and Savior! I am grateful for Your love that flows in my heart and soul. Bountiful blessings are mine, when I put my trust in You!

In Jesus' Name, Amen

February 21

Have You Looked to the Word of God for Your Answers?

Are you looking for answers to your life questions? Is your heart open to receive more of God's love? You are headed in the right direction when you take a step closer to God. He has written your name on the palms of His hands and is wanting to reach out and hold yours. He has given you truth to apply to your life. Open His Word and let His words of life resonate in your heart and be planted in your soul. The light you are seeking will be found as you come closer to Him through the Word of God. Open your Bible, pray for direction, and find the answers you are seeking with God! *"Your word is a lamp to my feet and a light to my path,"* Psalm 119:105.

Dear Lord,

Thank You for giving me the answers to my questions in Your words of wisdom. Your Word is a lamp to my feet as I walk with You. My path is clearer as I walk in the light of Your truth. I will keep listening as You *light up my life*!

In Jesus' Name, Amen

February 22

Are You Looking Up?

Are you facing a difficult challenge? Do you feel like you have too many sins to be forgiven? Is your strength gone and you need someone to lift you out of the dark? Look up to your Lord for the help you need! He will lift you up and encourage you with His love. Even when you think you have lost your way the Lord will encourage you to press on and give you the courage to stand tall. You will not fall when you are held up by the hand of the Lord! As you cry out to the Lord, let Psalm 121:1-2 come alive inside of you, "*I lift up my eyes to the hills. From where does my help come? My help comes from the Lord, who made heaven and earth.*"

Dear Lord,

I need Your help! There are things around me that hurt my heart and put burdens on my soul. I know that You will be there to lift me up each time I reach out for You! Your blessings will come as I turn back around, look up, take hold of Your hand, and fall into Your strong arms!

In Jesus' Name, Amen

February 23

Have You Prayed Boldly for What is on Your Heart?

There are prayers that need to be prayed. There are people in our lives God wants us to pray with and pray for. When we come together with one heart and soul, in one accord, we will find our prayers become bold and powerful. The Holy Spirit moves when people come together to pray from their heart. When two or more join their hearts in prayer, God is among them to hear and answer their bold prayers! *"Again I say to you, if two of you agree on earth about anything they ask, it will be done for them by my Father in heaven. For where two or three are gathered in my name, there am I among them,"* Matthew 18:19-20. Let us gather together and pray!

Dear Lord,

I am praying boldly today for what is on my heart. I will keep praying to You by myself and with others and believing that You will answer these prayers in Your timing and for Your glory!

In Jesus' name, Amen

February 24

Have You Let the Lord Build Your House?

We all have a choice about who we will follow and how we will live. We all have the chance to make the decision to invite the Lord to live with us and build our house. He is waiting for us to let Him in. He wants us to have the best life ever and that starts with our hearts wide open to live in His love. As we build our lives around the love of the Lord, we are able to love others as He has loved us. As we work to build our best life ever, we will allow the Lord to build our homes. Our labor is never in vain when we open the door wide to His love. *"Unless the Lord build the house, those who build it labor in vain,"* Psalm 127:1.

Dear Lord,

I will work as You desire so that You can build up my life. I will let You build my house, so my labor is not in vain. You are my foundation of hope and my source of peace. Thank You for building my home so peace can dwell in me!

In Jesus' Name, Amen

February 25

Do You Want to Live with a Heart for Others?

We live in a world with different opinions and backgrounds. We will not always agree, but we can always choose to love and extend grace to others. Let us all work to put aside our differences and come together in unity to love and respect one another. The Lord wants us to dwell together in love and forgiveness. He wants us to come together to pray and seek His will for our lives. He created us in His image to love and be loved! United together with hearts that are filled with the love of God is the way we can stand together. *"Behold, how good and pleasant it is when brothers dwell in unity!"* Psalm 133:1.

Dear Lord,

I pray a bold prayer for all to live united and not divided. I pray that I will love as You have loved me and forgive as You have forgiven me! I want to dwell in Your love and give grace to those in need of Your love and mercy.

In Jesus' Name, Amen

February 26

Are You Afraid to Speak Up About the Truth?

Are you wanting to speak up about the truth, but fear has kept you silent? Have you been relying on the Lord to help you or still letting fear stop you from speaking? When you let the Lord reign over you, peace will settle over you. With the Lord, all fear will go away, and faith will conquer all your fears. The Lord wants you to stand up for truth and not let others stop you from doing what is right. You do not have to worry that you will be alone because the Lord will be with you. You are one step away from truth. *"Do not be afraid, but go on speaking and do not be silent, for I am with you…"* Acts 18:9-10. Keep believing and let the Lord take all your fears!

Dear Lord,

I need Your guidance and help today. I want to speak up about the truth and make a difference for You as one of Your children. I hear you telling me, "Keep speaking the truth as you let your faith rise over fear and trust Me to be with you always." I will stand up fearlessly with You, Lord!

In Jesus' Name, Amen

February 27

Have You Given the Lord Your Heart?

Are you ready to see all that the Lord has for you? Do you hope that you can grow deeper faith as you worry less and trust more? Change starts on the inside as you give the Lord more of your heart. God wants you to trust Him and let go of your worries, so that you can grow! Let them go and trust the Lord to do something new in you. He has wonderful plans just for you. Open your heart and say *yes* to the perfect love of Jesus Christ so that He can share His vision for you!

Dear Lord,

I pray Psalm 139:23, "*Search me, O God, and know my heart! Try me and know my thoughts!*" As You search me, You will know I love you and want to grow even closer to You. As You try me, You will know my thoughts are on You and how I can live to please You more. You always want the best for me, so I will stop questioning and start trusting and obeying as I follow You with a devoted heart!

In Jesus' Name, Amen

February 28

Are You Living with the Power of God?

Are you living with the power of God? Do you believed in the gospel message of truth? Are you willing to surrender all to Jesus who gives you eternal life? Jesus has invited you to come to Him just as you are because He loves you so much. There is power in the name of Jesus to save everyone who believes! You can have this power when you choose to follow the Lord. Let His power come alive inside you as you trust Him. Your faith will bring you out of your pain into His arms of grace. He is waiting to welcome you into His kingdom that never ends!

Dear Lord,

I am praying Romans 1:16, *"For I am not ashamed of the gospel, for it is the power of God for salvation to everyone who believes…"* I know that You have come to save all who believe, and I am living with Your power in my life. Thank you for Your gospel which gives me hope! You have renewed me with Your Spirit of power and Your Word of Life.

In Jesus' Name, Amen

Monthly Reflections

As you pray and lean on the Lord's promises, write
what the Lord has revealed to you for this month.

I CAN DO
all things
THROUGH HIM
who gives me
strength.
PHILIPPIANS 4:13

March 1

Have You Called Upon the Lord?

Are you looking for guidance and encouragement? When you need help, you have a sovereign God there to help you whenever you call upon Him. Hasten your voice to the one who knows and hears everything. He will give ear to your prayers as you call upon Him. Pray and listen for His voice as He answers your cries for help. Turn to God and let God do it for you. You have been going at it by yourself for too long. It is time to let go and let God help you! The counsel you are seeking is just a prayer away!

Dear Lord,

I am praying Psalm 141:1 *"O LORD, I call upon you; hasten to me! Give ear to my voice when I call to you."* I am so thankful for Your guidance and encouragement. In the morning, You are there to enlighten me. In the daytime, I draw to You and feel Your joy in my soul. In the evening, I feel Your deep peace as You take care of my every need. You are always there for me!

In Jesus' Name, Amen

March 2

Do You Want to Feel the Presence of the Lord in Your Life?

Have you been living with the power of Jesus inside you? This power of the Holy Spirit is present in all believers who make the choice to follow Jesus. Surrender all to Him and activate the power of the Holy Spirit. He will guide you to all truth and empower you with His presence. As you do, you will feel His presence and power come alive in you. This life changing decision will change you from the inside out. Pray to let go and let God make you new. Listen, He is calling you!

Dear Lord,

I know You are calling me to draw closer. I am praying to see You more as I come closer to Your love. As I pray Psalm 144:5, *"Bow your heavens, O LORD, and come down!"* I feel Your power strengthening me! Your powerful presence is real and actively working inside me. The power of the Holy Spirit is guiding me and interceding for me as I pray. I am full of new hope today as I let You do new things in me!

In Jesus' Name, Amen

March 3

Have You Activated
the Holy Spirit Inside of You?

Have you activated the power of the Holy Spirit within you? Do you want to know the Holy Spirit, but have not let go of total control over your life? Have you said yes to the love of God, but do not know the Holy Spirit? As you have opened your heart to God's love through Jesus, He has poured His love upon you through the Holy Spirit who dwells in you to help and guide you. Say yes to more of His presence in your life by praying to receive Him. He will show you a freer way of living. As you welcome the Holy Spirit in your life, you will have a new friend who will change your life completely!

Dear Lord,

Thank You for the Holy Spirit's presence in my life. I feel encouraged as I read in Romans 5:5, *"God's love has been poured into our hearts through the Holy Spirit who has been given to us."* I am so grateful that I have the Holy Spirit working inside of me as I let go, listen, and obey the promptings that I hear from You.

In Jesus' Name, Amen

March 4

What Are You Setting Your Mind On?

Are you setting your mind on your problems or the solution? Have you lost hope because you cannot see an answer to your challenges? Keep listening to the Holy Spirit calling you closer. He is the answer you have been searching for. Your love for Jesus has set you apart, but now it is time to grow closer to the Holy Spirit so that you can live your best life. Life in the flesh has not brought you what you hoped for. You are restless and weary from relying on everyone and everything else to bring you peace and joy. You are plodding through life with your head down. Lift your head up and turn your heart towards the eternal love that awaits you in the Spirit! Welcome the Holy Spirit into your heart and find life and peace!

Dear Lord,

I am full of Your perfect peace as I allow the Spirit to work actively inside me. I cannot find life and peace without You! Your Truth is clear in Romans 8:6, "*To set the mind on the spirit is life and peace.*" With the Spirit in me, I have everything I need in You!

In Jesus' Name, Amen

March 5

Are You in Constant Prayer?

Are you rejoicing today for what God is doing in your life right now? Have you praised Him for what He has done in the past? Are you continuing to pray believing that God hears you? He has shown you His glory before and He will do it again. That mountain He moved for you, as you prayed believing in the promise, can be moved again. Do not fear or doubt but believe! God is greater than your problem! He loves you and will give you what you need as you pray more and worry less! Turn your worry list into a prayer list and keep praying from your heart!

Dear Lord,

I will keep praying for what is on my heart. I know that if I continue praying, believing that You will answer me, you will hear me and answer my prayers. I am clinging to the promise found in one of my favorite scriptures, Romans 12:12, *"Rejoice in hope, be patient in tribulation, be constant in prayer."* I know the answers to my prayers are coming as I continue rejoicing in hope, waiting patiently in tribulation, and praying without ceasing!

In Jesus' Name, Amen

March 6

Do You Have People in Your Life Who Bring You Closer to Christ?

Are you struggling? Have you isolated yourself from people God intended to be close to you? Are you discouraged because you do not have anyone in your life challenging you to grow closer to Christ? Seek the counsel and love of the Lord and ask Him to put these people in your life. He has given you family and friends who will sharpen you like iron sharpens iron. There are people who love you and want to help you. You will grow to be one who sharpens and encourages others. Find His love to give love. Start with the love of Christ and He will give you the friends you need!

Dear Lord,

Thank You for giving me iron-sharpening believers so we can pray for each other and build one another up! Help me to love, encourage, and sharpen others as I pray for them. Proverbs 27:17 gives me hope as I read," *Iron sharpens iron, and one man sharpens another."*

In Jesus' Name, Amen

March 7

Have You Let God in
This Season of Your Life?

There are seasons of change in our lives just like there are seasons of change in the weather. We have a choice about how we will live in each new season of life. We can choose to keep God, who never changes, or we can choose to live without Him as each new season comes. He wants to be present in each of us as we grow and change. He will set our hearts on fire as we remain close to Him. Turn toward the Lord and do not let another day go by without the warmth of the Son! He will warm you from the inside out every day no matter what the weather is like outside!

Dear Lord,

I know there will be seasons of change in my life, but I know that You will remain the same today, yesterday, and forever! The only way to live in each season of my life is to be more devoted to You. As I read Ecclesiastes 3:1, I am encouraged to hope; *"For everything there is a season, and a time for every matter under heaven."*

In Jesus' Name, Amen

March 8

Have You Lost Your Motivation for What You Have Been Called to Do?

We all have a purpose and a calling given to us by God. There are people in our lives that God wants us to team up with to do the work that is ours to finish. The task at hand can be daunting if we never reach out to others to work with us. When we feel like giving up, these people can help us get back on track. They lift us up and encourage us to keep going. God knows that two are better than one and so He gives us people who will stand by us to help finish the work before us. With God in the center, we can all be motivated to accomplish His purpose and blessings with our combined efforts!

Dear Lord,

I am humbled to be able to work with You and those you have given me to accomplish the tasks that You have purposed for me. Thank you for these people with like minds and hearts to help me as I toil. I will remember Your promise in Ecclesiastes 4:9, *"Two are better than one, because they have a good reward for their toil."*

In Jesus' Name, Amen

March 9

Have You Told Others What
God has Done for You?

Have you shared the truth of salvation with others? Do you know that the Lord can use you to spread His message of love and grace? Share the truth about the hope that is in you. Your testimony about what the Lord has done in your life will bring others to know Christ's redeeming love and grace. There are many who do not have a personal relationship with Jesus Christ. They need His love and want His grace, but they have not heard the truth. Be the one heart helping another heart as you share the message of hope through Jesus Christ. Tell about His power to save as you share your testimony of faith!

Dear Lord,

I know that You use ordinary people to share the good news of Your redeeming love and grace so I will keep sharing the truth with awe and wonder. I will boast about You as I tell others about how great You are! Your Word gives direction in 1 Corinthians 1:31, *"Let the one who boasts, boast in the Lord."*

In Jesus' Name, Amen

March 10

Have You Let Go of Fear so that You Can Hold Onto God?

When fear creeps into our lives, it can prevent us from growing our faith. Fear robs us of a closer relationship with our Lord. Fear makes us do things we regret. Fear is a liar! When fear sets in, it can stop us from doing what we have been called to do. The Lord knows we will face fear, so He has given us hope through His promise that He will never leave or forsake us. He is with us always! He gives us His hand to help us as we let go of our fear and put on more faith. Take hold of His strong hand to let go of all fear!

Dear Lord,

When fear tries to creep into my life, I will let it go. I surrender my worries and fears of what might happen and replace it with more faith. I am clinging to the hope found in Isaiah 41:13 as I hear you tell me, *"For I, the LORD your God, hold your right hand; it is I who say to you, 'Fear not, I am the one who helps you'."*

In Jesus' Name, Amen

March 11

Do You Know that You Are God's Masterpiece of Beauty?

We are all created by God as a masterpiece of beauty in His image. Praise the Lord that He made each of us with unique attributes and talents! We are all beautiful in His eyes. The Lord sees into our souls and He knows our hearts and our minds. Our bodies are His temple where His Spirit dwells within us. How amazing is *this*? We are loved just as we are! As we believe and accept His love, our hearts are infused with His joy and our souls are filled with His hope! We are God's masterpieces!

Dear Lord,

I know that You made me in Your image. You know everything about me. Only You can see into my soul and know my heart. You even know my thoughts before they come to my mind. Your love has changed me from the inside out. I know you love me! As I read in 1 Corinthians 3:16, I am filled with Your promise of hope. *"Do you know that you are God's temple and that God's Spirit dwells in you?"*

In Jesus' Name, Amen

March 12

Are You Ready to Go
When You Are Called?

There are voices calling you in different directions. You can get distracted if you are not in tune with the frequency of God's voice. To hear His voice, be still and let Him into your heart. Are you listening to the Lord calling you? As you pray, let go and lay it all down to your loving God. He will direct you when you listen. You have been praying for a while now. However, you have not acted in faith because you do not see all the details. Do not question when you hear His voice but step out confidently in faith. Let go, rise up, and serve as you are called!

Dear Lord,

I have heard Your voice as I sit still and pray. You need more laborers in the fields that are full of people who need to hear about Your saving grace and steadfast love. Just as Isaiah was ready to go when called, we must be ready. Isaiah 6:8 encourages me; *"And I heard the voice of the Lord saying, "Whom shall I send and who will go for us?' Then I said, 'Here I am! Send me!'"*

In Jesus' Name, Amen

March 13

Are You Drawing Joy from the Wells of Salvation?

There are difficulties we must go through that we do not understand. We suffer heartache and we endure pain. There are people in our lives we loved who are gone and we miss them. Who can help mend our broken hearts? Jesus can help us. He heals and binds up our wounds. He is near to those who call upon Him. He knows our pain and weeps with us. But amidst our struggles, He brings joy! There is joy in the wells of His salvation as we know we will see our loved ones who are in Heaven with Him! Hallelujah! Jesus saves!

Dear Lord,

I miss people who are no longer in my life. I am sad when I think about them and how much I wish I could hug them and say "I love you" again. But I am at peace knowing they are completely healed in Your presence! They are experiencing the joy of Heaven! I have eternal hope that I will see them again one day! *"With joy you will draw water from the wells of salvation,"* Isaiah 12:3.

In Jesus' Name, Amen

March 14

Do You Know God's Love
for You Never Ends?

Are you ready to experience a true love that is patient and kind? How about love that is real and genuine? Do you want to feel special and loved, but you think you are unworthy? If you are looking for this kind of love that never ends, look to Jesus. Let His love in your heart! He has been waiting for you to come home to Him so that He can forgive and embrace you! He is patient and kind towards You. As you let Him in your heart, your heart will fill up with the sweet love of God and your love for others will beautifully blossom! Let God's love in and bloom where He plants you!

Dear Lord,

Thank You for loving me with patience and kindness. I feel Your love covering every part of me as I let go and let You in my whole heart. It is so refreshing to know this kind of pure and genuine love. Your love never ends! *"Love is patient and kind; love does not envy or boast; it is not arrogant,"* 1 Corinthians 13:4.

In Jesus' Name, Amen

March 15

Are You Standing Firm in the Faith?

Are you standing up for what Christ has put in your heart? When you are tested, are you standing firm in your faith and living out what you believe? You have been given Jesus to receive love and to extend love to others. He wants you to keep living out what you believe as you walk daily. Live out your beliefs so that you can make a difference in the lives of other people. People need to see Jesus in you! Just as Jesus has been compassionate and kind towards you, be that way towards those around you. Extend grace and give love. As you abide in the love and grace of Jesus, you will be enriched and able to stand firm in your faith!

Dear Lord,

It is refreshing to know I can stand firm in my faith when I have You as my firm foundation. You have set the example for me to follow. As I read Your Word and pray daily, I am enriched in every way by You! "*Be watchful, stand firm in the faith, act like men, be strong. Let all that you do be done in love,*" 1 Corinthians 16:13-14.

In Jesus' Name, Amen

March 16

Are You Saying Yes to God?

When you say yes to God, your life will change, and you will become brand new. You are reborn with His joyful Spirit inside! You are free to love and live victoriously with a Savior by your side and in your heart. Let go of what is holding you back and say yes to God! He has already said *yes* to you!

Dear Lord,

I am so glad I said Yes to life with You years ago. I know what life is like with You and without You. The first part of my life was lived without knowing You as my Savior. I was searching for someone or something to fill the void in my heart. As I heard about Your eternal love and amazing grace, and decided to follow You, I found a lasting joy and my life was changed the day I said yes! Every day with You is sweeter than the day before! My soul is alive, and my heart is on fire with the love spark of Jesus and the Holy Spirit. As I read 2 Corinthians 1:20, I will say *yes* again and again, *"For all the promises of God find their Yes in him."*

In Jesus' Name, Amen

March 17

Did You Know that God has Engraved You on the Palms of His Hands?

The Lord has called you, dear one. He has engraved you in the palms of His hands. He has set you apart to love and serve Him. He needs you to see Him and let Him in your heart. You have been walking alone and it has worn you out. You need help but do not know where to turn. The pressures of life have certainly weighed on your heart and you are struggling. Look up and see the Lord with open arms ready to revive you!

Dear Lord,

I will not take my eyes off You, Lord, but I will keep looking up and keep my focus on You. Thank You for meeting my every need and helping me right when I need You. Thank you for the truth in Isaiah 49:16 that speaks to my heart. *"Behold, I have engraved you on the palms of my hands."* You know me and love every part of me! I am so thankful for Your amazing love that gives me strength and courage to press on! I will run to You, my Lord and King!

In Jesus' Name, Amen

March 18

Are You Giving Bountifully
from Your Heart?

You have a choice about how you will give to others and if you will give. People need your love, and you have opportunities to help sow seeds of love into other people. It all starts in your heart. You have been made by God out of love, with a heart to love, so that you can *give* love. As you love, you spread seeds of hope to those around you. Are you sowing seeds bountifully with a grateful heart?

Dear Lord,

Oh, how I thank You for showing me where You need me. I will keep serving as You call me. Your love has lifted me up to see the needs around me. I will keep sowing seeds to spread the fragrance of Your love to those around me. Bountiful seeds will bloom beautifully in the hearts of Your people as You water them. Thank You for giving the growth in all our hearts! *"Whoever sows sparingly will also reap sparingly, and whoever sows bountifully will also reap bountifully,"* 2 Corinthians 9:6.

In Jesus' Name, Amen

March 19

Are You Seeking the Lord While He is Near to You?

Are you searching for the Lord? He is near to all who want a relationship with Him. Have you felt His touch upon your heart? Seek Him with all your heart and let Him change you by His life-giving power! Jesus transforms all who invite Him to live in their hearts. Come closer to His heart and feel the freedom that He gives you. He paid the price for you as your sins were washed away by His blood! Come nearer, as He has much to show you, dear one.

Dear Lord,

Thank You for the freedom that is mine in You! I am coming closer to Your heart each day as I live in Your love and set my hope on You. You have set me free and I am celebrating my life in Christ! I am calling on You for more help and guidance. Thank You for hearing my prayers as I draw nearer to You. I am comforted by Isaiah 55:6," *Seek the Lord while he may be found, call upon him while he is near.*" Come near to me Lord Jesus!

In Jesus' Name, Amen

March 20

Did You Know the Hand
of the Lord is on You?

We all have prayers on our heart. As we pray them, our loving God listens with His hand upon our hearts. He is ready to give us what we need as we come to the throne of grace with our hearts wide open! Maybe we do not have because we do not ask, believing that God will answer us. Are our prayers prayed out of faith or are we just going through the motions? Do we trust that God knows what we need and will work things out for our good and His glory? Start trusting and see God's hand upon you!

Dear Lord,

I know that You hear all my prayers. Your hand is upon me and as I pray. Thank You for giving me hope as I believe You will work all things out for Your glory. I am going to quit worrying and continue praying from my heart! Your hand saves me! You hear me! I am full of hope as I read in Isaiah 59:1, *"Behold, the LORD's hand is not shortened, that it cannot save, or his ear dull, that it cannot hear."*

In Jesus' Name, Amen

March 21

Do You Want a Constant Companion to Always be with You?

When we accept Jesus Christ as our Savior, we receive the Holy Spirit who lives inside of us. As we live by the Spirit, something amazing happens! Our lives are empowered by the same Spirit that raised Jesus from the dead! We have new life in Christ and a constant companion in the Holy Spirit! We will also have a friend who is always with us to guide us each step of the way. Live by the Spirit to keep in step with Him. Listen, wait for the Spirit to prompt you, and stay in step with the Spirit as the road ahead will take you on a magnificent and amazing journey!

Dear Lord,

I want to thank You for the Holy Spirit, my constant companion, who guides me to all truth and helps me make the best decisions! I am most grateful for His power that lives inside of me! I will never get out of step when I listen and obey His voice of truth! As I read Galatians 5:25, I am encouraged, *"If we live by the Spirit, let us also keep in step with the Spirit."*

In Jesus' Name, Amen

March 22

Have You Given Up Before the Fruit Ripens?

Are you growing weary of doing good? Have you lost the zeal and determination you once had? Are you struggling to see any fruit from your work? There are times when you will feel weary and tired. God knows that these times will come, so He has given you the Holy Spirit to give extra strength to help you. Your Strengthener will help you push through the hard times so that you can keep going. Listen to Him and stay on track. You are needed and your work is not in vain. Seeds are being planted. You will reap if you do not give up! Keep working for the Lord to see the good fruit!

Dear Lord,

The season of reaping will come if I do not grow weary. Thank You for Your good fruit that will come in due time! Thank you for the Holy Spirit to help me to continue reaching out with Your added strength to spread seeds of love. *"And let us not grow weary of doing good, for in due season, we will reap, if we do not give up,"* Galatians 6:9.

In Jesus' Name, Amen

March 23

Did You Know You Are
Sealed with the Holy Spirit?

When you believe in Jesus as your Savior, you receive the gift of the promised Holy Spirit. This Spirit is the same Spirit that lives in Jesus! As Jesus was baptized, the Spirit descended upon Him. As you are baptized into Christ, your new life is guaranteed in Him and you are sealed with His promised Holy Spirit! Yield to the Holy Spirit, who is Jesus in you, and you will be recharged and fully awakened to new life! He will light up your life like never before! Say yes to Jesus and let Him give you this treasured gift that will change you from the inside out!

Dear Lord,

I am wide awake to You as I have turned on the light in my life. I just needed to activate Your power inside me by yielding all to You. As I did, You have awakened me to new life and given me new joy and an overwhelming peace! *"In him you also, when you heard the word of truth, the gospel of your salvation, and believed in him, were sealed with the promised Holy Spirit,"* Ephesians 1:13.

In Jesus' Name, Amen

March 24

Do You Need Help
with Words to Speak and Pray?

Are you struggling with what you need to say to that person on your heart? Have you been worrying about how to tell them what they need to hear from you? Are you too overwhelmed that you cannot find the words to pray? Trust the Lord to give you the words to speak and pray. He will put His words in your mouth as you open it up to let Him fill it. As you grow closer to the Lord, He will fill your heart and you will receive all that He wants to give you. When your heart is open, you will know how to pray for others. The Lord will give you the words. Pray in the Spirit and let the Lord put His words on your tongue!

Dear Lord,

I am so grateful that I have you, Lord, to help me as I speak. I will seek Your counsel by praying for your words to say. I am not afraid when I have Your help. Only You can calm my anxious heart! "*And the LORD said to me, "Behold, I have put my words in your mouth*," Jeremiah 1:9.

In Jesus' Name, Amen

March 25

Are You Living with All
Your Spiritual Blessings in Christ?

Are you living with all your spiritual blessings in Christ? You have His Spirit within you as you gave your heart to Christ. As a believer, God can do more in you when you are fully living in His power that is already present in you. When you activate this power in your life, you will know the riches of His eternal love and the hope of your calling through Jesus Christ! Be active by letting the power that resides in you work in you. Trust Him to do more in you than you could ever dream or imagine! When you do, you will experience revival in your heart and soul!

Dear Lord,

I am sealed with the Holy Spirit. I am living actively in Your power within me so that You can do more in me than I could ever do on my own. I have joy that has flooded my entire being! Ephesians 3:20 has come to life, *"Now to him who is able to do far more abundantly than all we ask or think, according to the power at work within us."*

In Jesus' Name, Amen

March 26

Are You Living with an Open Heart to Hope?

Are you feeling lonely? Have you been working alone and have just about given up? Do you need help to do what you know you have been called to do? Come to Jesus Christ and let Him fully awaken you to new life. When you open your heart to Christ, He will strengthen and encourage you to do what He needs you to do. You can be one with Christ as one body and one Spirit as you trust and obey Him. Yield to Him and give faith a fighting chance. God is fighting for you!

Dear Lord,

You are my eternal hope! I gave You my heart years ago and know what it is like to be redeemed! There is a oneness with You that fills my heart with peace and makes me rejoice! I am listening as I live in fullness with Your Spirit inside of me! I am one in Christ! It is well with My soul! Ephesians 4:4 encourages me as I read, *"There is one body and one Spirit— just as you were called to one hope the belongs to your call…"*

In Jesus' Name, Amen

March 27

Are You Calling Upon the Lord?

Are you feeling hopeless? Do you feel like there is no one who can understand you or what you are going through right now? The Lord wants you to pray for what is on your heart. *One hundred percent of the prayers not prayed will not be answered!* The Lord wants you to keep praying! He sees your challenge and has compassion on you. As you call upon the Lord, He will show you His glory and wrap His outstretched arms around you! Let the Lord comfort you and give you hope!

Dear Lord,

I am so humbled and blessed by Your presence in my life. I know that there has not been a prayer that You have not heard and answered in Your will and timing. I will keep seeking Your counsel and comfort. As I call upon You, I will hear Your gentle whisper and You will tell me great and hidden things that You want me to know. I am encouraged by Jeremiah 33:3, *"Call to me and I will answer you, and tell you great and hidden things that you have not known."*

In Jesus' Name, Amen

March 28

Is Your Armor on?

Are you needing strength today? Are you growing tired and weary from all the stress you're facing? Let go of your stress and hold onto the Lord. Call upon the Him and let the Lord strengthen you! Take off fear and put on the armor of God that will protect you from harm. Those things meant for your harm will be turned for good by the Lord who watches over you. There is hope for you as you come to the Lord. He will give you all that you need right when you need it! Prayers up and armor on!

Dear Lord,

I will let go of my worries and fears and put my armor on. Your strength covers me when I am weak. I will be strong in You, my Lord! I am thankful for Your love that takes away all my fears and never ends! I will keep praying and relying on You, Lord! Nothing is impossible for You! *"Finally, be strong in the Lord and in the strength of his might."* Ephesians 6:10

In Jesus Name, Amen

March 29

Who is Your King?

Is the Lord your King? He has come to be King over all. He will never leave or forsake you, dear one. He loves you and will take you back. There is nothing you have done that will make Him love you less. Hear Him gently whispering to you as He speaks, "Come to me with your heart wide open so that I can fill you with my love. You are worthy and loved, my dear child." Do you believe that He loves you? Come back home and rest in His arms of grace. *"And the LORD will be King over all the earth. On that day, the LORD will be one and His name one,"* Zechariah 14:9.

Dear Lord,

I do believe that You love me. I hear You are calling me, and I will come to You, my one true King! In Your presence, I am full of joy as I listen to Your love for me. Thank You for speaking love into my heart as I praise You, my Lord!

In Jesus' Name, Amen

March 30

What Goal Are You Pressing on Towards?

Are you straining forward by yourself? Have you pressed on in the past, but are now tired and have lost your dedication and drive? When you make Jesus your goal and let Him work inside of you to accomplish all the work, He will do mighty things *in* and *through* you! Make His love your reality and not a possibility. Give up the things that are taking You away from God and open your heart up to what He wants to do *in* you! You will see your goals change to include the plans and purposes created for you by God! He is calling you to keep your eyes on Him!

Dear Lord,

You are my goal and my prize. I am whole in You as I let You work inside of me with the fire of the Holy Spirit burning brightly within me! My heart is on fire for You, my Lord and Savior! I will press on with You as I read from Philippians 3:14, *"I press on toward the goal for the prize of the upward call of God in Christ Jesus."*

In Jesus' Name, Amen

March 31

Why Are You Anxious?

Are you worried about things you cannot change? Are you fearful about your future? Is your soul heavy with various cares and concerns? Take these thoughts captive and let God fill you with hope. He loves you and promises to help you as you pray about what is on your heart. Let go of fear and let God's peace settle in your heart. Listen to the love of God as you pray about the things you cannot change. He can change what seems impossible as you let go and let Him answer your prayers! Cry out to the Lord and tell Him your concerns! *"Do not be anxious about anything, but in everything by prayer and supplication with thanksgiving let your requests be made known to God,"* Philippians 4:6.

Dear Lord,

I know You will give me peace as I pray about what is on my heart. My soul will be comforted and refreshed by You as I let go and let You help me. Only You can calm my anxious heart as I let Your peace settle over me. My worries have disappeared as I pray to You, my Prince of Peace!

In Jesus' Name, Amen

Monthly Reflections

As you pray and lean on the Lord's promises, write
what the Lord has revealed to you for this month.

HE IS NOT HERE,

for he has

RISEN,

as he said.

COME,

see the place

where he lay.

MATTHEW 28:6

April 1

Do You Need to be Made New in Christ?

Are you sure of your salvation? If you are not sure of where you will spend eternity, be sure today! Salvation is available for all who believe! Confess with your mouth that you are a sinner in need of a Savior and believe in your heart that Jesus died for you so that you will have eternal life! Let Jesus reign in your heart. He has been waiting for you to let Him in so He can make you a new creation! If you choose Him, you will have peace and joy in your heart right now and will spend eternity in heaven! Search your heart and be confident of your salvation!

Dear Lord,

Thank You for making me a new creation as I remember the moment I first let You touch my heart! The old self has died, the new has come! My heart is full of joy and peace that no one can take away! As I believed, You changed me! 2 Corinthians 5:17 has come to life. *"Therefore, if anyone is in Christ, he is a new creation. The old has passed away; behold, the new has come."*

In Jesus' Name, Amen

April 2

Have You Claimed the Victory that is Yours in Jesus Christ?

Jesus Christ gives you victory as you claim your citizenship in His Kingdom by believing in Him. He has given you victory over sin when you believe *and* repent. You have this choice and privilege to love and honor Him. When you do, you will be victorious! The proof of His love is found at the cross where He died for you! He needs you to let go and let Him fight your battle of the mind. Align your heart with His love and Jesus will give you faith-filled eyes to see with new vision!

Dear Lord,

My heart is filled with new joy and thanksgiving every time I think of how much You love me! I am forgiven and free to claim the victory in You, Jesus, my Savior forever, as you walk with me and talk with me in relationship. I am living victoriously when I love and trust You with all my heart! There is victory in Jesus! 1 Corinthians 15:57,*"Thanks be to God, who gives us victory through our Lord Jesus Christ."*

In Jesus' Name, Amen

April 3

Are You Still Trusting the Lord?

Are you trusting the Lord with all your heart? Do you believe that God has a greater plan for you, or are you leaning on your own understanding? You may be struggling with how things might turn out but remember that God is always faithful! He has a plan that will bring you closer to His love. There will be times of great joy that follow your trail of tears. Believe in the promise of His rainbow behind your rain cloud. The Son will shine upon you as you keep trusting the Lord with all your heart!

Dear Lord,

I do not know how things will turn out. But I do know that You will direct my path as I follow the command in Proverbs 3:5, *"Trust in the Lord with all of your heart, and do not lean on your own understanding."* My faith is stronger each day when I keep trusting You even when I do not understand. I will keep my faith in You as I keep faithfully and fervently praying for what is on my heart. Thank You for always being faithful to me!

In Jesus' Name, Amen

April 4

Have You Prayed to Grow
Closer to the Lord?

The Lord hears our prayers. He attunes His ear to the sound of our voices as we pray. And when we do not have the words to pray, the Holy Spirit intercedes for us as we bow down to the Lord to pray from our heart. *We cannot get answers to prayers that are not prayed.* Instead of giving up, keep praying even when it seems impossible. Just because the answer has not come, does not mean that God does not hear our prayers. As we keep praying from our heart, our relationship with the Lord deepens and matures and our faith definitely grows!

Dear Lord,

Thank You for hearing my prayers as I pray to you. You are present in my life when I keep close to you. I will keep praying Psalm 143:1, *"Hear my prayer, O LORD; give ear to my pleas for mercy!"* I love to pray to You and tell You not only my pleas but also my praises! You are the one true King of my heart! In Your presence I find rest and peace!

In Jesus' Name, Amen

April 5

Did You Know that You Have an Inheritance in God?

Are you setting your mind on the heavenly things above which cannot be destroyed or devalued? Is your heart connected to Jesus Christ who has paid the price for your sins? He has set you free to live differently from the world and its ways. You are set apart as a child of the living God with an inheritance of the saints of light when you believed and followed Him to life and peace. Life with Him in the Spirit is full of peace, love, hope, and joy! Live the life you were intended to live with your inheritance in Christ!

Dear Lord,

I want to praise and thank You for your glorious presence in and around me. I know that I am Your child because I have genuinely believed! As I read truth in Your Word and set my heart on You, I am rich indeed! I have my inheritance in You for which I am most grateful! Colossians 1:12 encourages me, *"Giving thanks to the Father, who has qualified you to share in the inheritance of the saints in light."*

In Jesus' Name, Amen

April 6

Are You Looking for the Peace of Christ to Rule in Your Heart?

Are you looking for peace? Have you looked to the Lord for help with what is bothering you right now? Seek His face and counsel. Trust the Lord and let His peace flow like a beautiful river and calm the rough waters in your soul. When you call upon Him, the peace of Christ will flow in and through you. His light will shine in the darkest moments right when you need it. Open your heart and let the peace of Christ rule in your heart!

Dear Lord,

I am basking in Your peace that comforts me deep down in my soul. Even when the world around me is divided, I am at peace within my soul. The best decision I ever made was trusting You with all my heart. The moment I did, peace entered my life. Now, Your peace rules inside me. Colossians 3:15 promises peace, and I feel alive as I read it, *"And let the peace of Christ rule in your hearts, to which indeed you were called in one body. And be thankful."*

In Jesus' Name, Amen

April 7

Have You Thanked God for the People He has Given You to Love?

Have you thanked God for His blessings in your life? Have you praised Him for the people that He has given you to love? There are so many who love and care about you. God knows we all need love. In fact, He loves you so much that He has given you Jesus to live inside of you when you make Him Lord of your life. The Holy Spirit inside of you will bless you richly when you let His love into your heart and soul!

Dear Lord,

I am so thankful for You and am blessed beyond measure because of Your love for me! I know Your love remains as You are in me. Thank You for my family and friends who love me. I lift them all up in prayer as I praise You for their love! Keep them close to Your heart, Lord. I will keep them close to mine as I keep praying and praising You! 1 Thessalonians 1:2 reminds me to keep praying as I read, *"We give thanks to God always for all of you, constantly mentioning you in our prayers."*

In Jesus' Name, Amen

April 8

Have You Let God Put His Shield of Love and Protection Around You?

Are you struggling alone as your problems are rising? Have you lost your hope because things you are facing now seem impossible with no solution? Are you looking for the key to unlock the door to greater hope? Jesus Christ is the key you have been looking for. He is the way to the Father. He will give you life because He is the way-maker! Seek His truth and open the door to life! He will surround you with grace and live inside you. He is a shield around you and the lifter of your head! Move out of the dark and walk into the light of His glorious love!

Dear Lord,

I know the key to greater hope and life is found in You. I can open the door to the new life You want for me as I experience all of the fullness of Christ and the power of the Holy Spirit! I am soaring with joy as I read the truth in Psalm 5:12, *"For you bless the righteous, O LORD; you cover him with favor as with a shield."*

In Jesus' Name, Amen

April 9

Do You Believe that God Will Do What He Says He Will Do?

Have you let God in so that He can do something new in you? He is faithful and will surely transform you when you surrender all. Are you filled with the hope of God or fear and doubt because of what you see? Faith is being sure of what you hope for, without reservation, even when you do not see. Take another step and trust God to remain faithful to you. As you are obedient to His will, He will be with you every step of the way. God is always faithful, and He will do what He has promised you. Will you do what He asks of you?

Dear Lord,

You have challenged me to step out of my comfort zone into Your will for me. I will be obedient to You as You have called me so I can hear you say, "Well done, my good and faithful servant." My faith has brought me closer to You with each step I have taken. Thank You for always being faithful to me! *"He who calls you is faithful; he will surely do it,"* 1 Thessalonians 5:24.

In Jesus' Name, Amen

April 10

Are You Focusing on the Goodness of God?

Your Lord will keep you from all evil. When the Lord reigns in You, you are protected. Angels surround you and minister to you as you keep close to the Lord! Whispers of love are all around you as you listen to God's voice. Do you hear Him telling you He loves you and will never leave you? Listen closely and be encouraged as He keeps you safe. *"The Lord will keep you from all evil; he will keep your life,"* Psalm 121:7.

Dear Lord,

As I pray today, I am enlightened and encouraged by Your love and Your goodness. I am listening with wonder and awe to Your love for me, and I am basking in Your glory and majesty! You are my Lord, and nothing can ever separate me from You and Your love! I am comforted and protected when I am in Your presence. There is peace in the stillness of my soul as I sit at Your feet and worship You, my glorious King!

In Jesus' Name, Amen

April 11

Is Your Heart Broken?

The Lord directs our hearts to His love when we open our hearts to Him. When we let go of our problems and hold on to Christ, we experience His steadfast love. He helps us when we are broken and puts the pieces of our hearts back together when we lean on Him. There are vast amounts of problems around us, but with God on our side and in our hearts, we will be victorious! He puts the pieces back together when Christ dwells in our minds and in our hearts. His steadfast love seals us with the Holy Spirit!

Dear Lord,

Thank You for loving me with a steadfast love! I am at peace when I let Your love cover every part of me. My fear disappears as I trust You even more. Thank You for rescuing me from the problems around me. I will not let them take over but will keep praying and leaning on You. 2 Thessalonians 3:5 is so real to me as I keep You close at heart, *"May the Lord direct your hearts to the love of God and to the steadfastness of Christ."*

In Jesus' Name, Amen

April 12

Are You Using Your God-Given Gifts?

Have you realized that you have been blessed with gifts from God? In fact, *you* are His gift! Jesus lives inside you when you make Him Lord of your life! God wants to redeem you and show you His vast blessings. He has given you spiritual gifts to use for your good and His glory! Surrender all to Him and use these gifts as they have been given to You. He gives you spiritual blessings when He seals you with the Holy Spirit. This gift of power from God, through Jesus Christ, is yours when you believe!

Dear Lord,

Thank You for Your glorious gifts and special blessings from heaven above! I will use the gifts You have given me by trusting You first and then obeying all that You ask of me. Good and perfect things come down from heaven when we use these gifts. I am Your beloved child who You have made in Your image. Thank You for creating me and giving me gifts as I live in relationship with You! I will obey 1 Timothy 4:14, *"Do not neglect the gift you have…"*

In Jesus' Name, Amen

April 13

Are You Fighting the Good Fight of Faith?

You will face issues in life that stir you up. Some will challenge you to fight back. You can either step up with God or be stepped on without Him. God will fight for you when you let Him into your life. Let Him fight your battle. He cannot be stopped and will win every time! Surrender all and see how God will step in and be victorious for you. Your fight is the good fight of the faith! Fight the good fight of the faith with God to be victorious!

Dear Lord,

Thank You for stepping in and fighting for me. I am letting go of fear and worry so that You can do a new thing in me. I will not let fear take over but will allow Your love to cover every part of me. I am not running on empty but am filled with Your power and strength! My fight is the good fight of the faith! 1 Timothy 6:12 has encouraged me to press on, *"Fight the good fight of the faith."*

In Jesus' Name, Amen

April 14

Are You Getting Your Strength from the Lord?

Are you about to give up? Is the weariness and weakness from your problems settling in your heart? Are you discouraged and disappointed about what you see around you? Turn to the Lord and let His power shine upon you and energize you. He will reign in you when you let Him into your soul. He has much to show you and wants to be a present power source for you. Turn up the power of God's grace given to you and draw on His strength. His presence of glory can be a real power source in your life!

Dear Lord,

I have seen Your glory all around me. I have let Your powerful presence reign in my heart as I have relied on You. My strength is in You, Lord! I will keep pressing on with You by my side, no matter what is before me. I can do all things with You who strengthen me! Thank You for loving me. I will keep loving You. Psalm 18:1 begins with these beautiful words, *"I love you, O LORD, my strength."*

In Jesus' Name, Amen

April 15

Are You Quenching the Holy Spirit with Your Words?

Are you struggling with the temptation to speak out against someone who has hurt you? Is the anger welling up inside you and you feel like you are about to explode? Did you know that your words spoken out from an offended heart can quench the Holy Spirit? You need to pray first and seek His counsel. God knows your pain and sees how others have hurt you. Before you speak out, talk to your loving God who loves you! Read, pray, and write a love letter to God so the words that you speak please the Lord and others.

Dear Lord,

Help me to speak words of encouragement and love to build others up. We all need to know we are loved. Before I speak, I will pray and seek Your counsel for the right words. I will meditate on Your Word so that I can hear You speaking to me. I am praying Psalm 19:14, *"Let the words of my mouth and the meditation of my heart be acceptable in your sight, O LORD, my rock and my redeemer."*

In Jesus' Name, Amen

April 16

Have You Prayed to the Lord for Your Heart's Desire?

The Lord is waiting for us to tell Him our hearts' desires when we pray. He has answers waiting for us that only He knows. We must ask and pray, sharing our desires while also seeking His will for our lives. Sometimes we do not have, because we are too afraid to ask. When the answer is no, the Lord has a better plan for us. When He is silent, keep praying persistently. His timing is perfect. God *answers* every prayer. He *hears* every prayer. He knows the desires of our hearts. He knows the plans He has for us! Keep praying in faith!

Dear Lord,

I will keep praying about what is on my heart. I will not stop praying for revival for all! You want all of our hearts so You can revive us again! Your plans will be fulfilled when we all pray as one with persistent faith! I believe Your promises in Psalm 20:4, *"May he grant you your heart's desire and fulfill all your plans!"* Let it be, Lord! Revive us again!

In Jesus' Name, Amen

April 17

Who is Your Shepherd?

We have a Good Shepherd who leads us to green pastures of hope and leads us beside still waters of peace. He is with us wherever we go when we make Him the Lord of our lives. We have no need to worry when we cling to His truth. When we follow Him, our fears of what might happen disappear. Our worries fade. The Lord will never lead us astray! We will never be lost when we trust more and want less. Trust the Good Shepherd, Jesus Christ!

Dear Lord,

Oh, how I love You! I do not want for anything else when I have You close at heart. You have brightened my life with hope and blessed me with peace even in the most difficult circumstances! You have met my wants and desires when I let You lead me. I will keep trusting You and clinging to Your Word. My faith is greater than my fear when I enter Your door to life and stay in Your sheepfold of protection. How can I want when I have You? My heart is content as I pray Psalm 23:1, *"The Lord is my shepherd; I shall not want."*

In Jesus' Name, Amen

April 18

Are You Thriving with Peace?

We all thrive when peace is present. We long for a place where we can feel peace. The peace of Christ rules in our lives when we give Him our hearts. He deposits peace inside of us as we make Him the Lord of our lives. He wraps us in His perfect peace as we let Him live in us. If we want to see peace around us, let us be a peacemaker. We will sow peace, as we make peace, by loving and forgiving those who have hurt us. We will see a harvest of righteousness when we sow peace instead of discord. Live out the truth in James 3:18, "*And a harvest of righteousness is sown in peace by those who make peace.*" We will see peace on Earth when we let the peace of Christ rule in our hearts!

Dear Lord,

I want to live in peace and will strive to make peace with those around me. It is Your desire that all live peacefully with one another. I will choose peace to make peace! Thank You for giving me peace so that I can thrive with peace!

In Jesus' Name, Amen

April 19

Are You Walking in Fear?

Are you walking around in fear? Have you lost your hope because you are afraid of what might happen? Is darkness surrounding you? Step out of the dark and into the light of the love of the Lord! He has come to take away all your fears! Let your faith be bigger than your fears as you trust and obey the Lord. His peace will calm your soul and take away your worries and fears. Let Psalm 27:1 resonate in you, *"The LORD is my light and my salvation; whom shall I fear?"*

Dear Lord,

You are my light and my salvation. I will not fear. I will trust You in all circumstances and acknowledge You in all ways. I will obey Your call to serve and be ready in and out of season to spread the good news of Your great love! Thank You for giving me abundant life when I chose to believe and follow You! I will humble myself before You and trust You even when I do not understand. O Lord, my King, my fears are gone, and it is well with my soul!

In Jesus' Name, Amen

April 20

Did You Know the Lord is Your Hiding Place

When you need comfort and rest, you can escape to a place of refuge with the Lord. He is your hiding place where you can get away from the problems that surround you. He comforts you with His calm and peaceful presence. Your sorrows will turn to joy when you let Him fill the empty places of your heart with His love! Shout with deliverance and let Him lead you to victory! Take the first step by saying *yes* to your Maker, the Master of your life!

Dear Lord,

You want me to find refuge in Your arms of protection so You can strengthen and comfort me! My fears vanish as soon as I step into faith with You by my side. There is nothing anyone can do to me to separate me from Your love! Nothing can come between You and me! Your love is so powerful and real in my life. Psalm 32:7 gives me hope as I pray Your promise, *"You are a hiding place for me; you preserve me from trouble; you surround me with shouts of deliverance."*

In Jesus' Name, Amen

April 21

Who is Lord of Your Life?

You receive countless blessings from God when He is Lord of your life. He wants a relationship with you and wants to live within you. He invites you to take His hand as He leads you to freedom. New life is possible when you obey and step into faith with hope from the Lord Jesus Christ! He gives you the Holy Spirit to live within you when you believe and love Him with all your heart, soul, and mind! Blessings abound in those who follow Christ!

Dear Lord,

The abundant blessings You give to those who follow You are countless! Your love has brightened my life with joy, peace, and hope that only comes from You! My heart is full of promise as I stand on Your promises! I believe my prayers will be answered as I keep praying faithfully even when I cannot see the path ahead. I will persistently pray with hope as I remember You love me! 1 Peter 1:8, *"Though you have not seen him, you love him…"*

In Jesus' Name, Amen

April 22

Are You Devoted to the Lord?

Where our heart is, our devotion will be greatest. When our hearts are devoted to God, He will give us the desires of our heart. As we delight in the Lord, our desires will become His desires for us. How can we delight in the Lord? By loving Him with all our heart, soul, and mind. Why do we need to be devoted to Him? When we fully love Him, we will know a love that fills us, and we can live in complete joy and peace. When we focus on Christ and live for Him, He will show us great and mighty things! *"Delight yourself in the LORD, and he will give you the desires of your heart,"* Psalm 37:4.

Dear Lord,

As I delight in you more each day, You are the desire of my heart. I want to live for You so that my life is full of Your goodness and grace. You have filled me with a joy that never leaves me and a peace that passes all my understanding. I delight in You! You are the desire of my heart!

In Jesus' Name, Amen

April 23

Are You Living in the Radiance of the Lord?

Are you ready to be revived with the radiance of the Lord? Do you want to be restored to new life? Look to the Lord, your God, and He will transform your heart and renew your mind. You will have a new passion to serve as you love the Lord with all your heart, soul, and mind. He will shine within you to bring the light to all the dark places around you. Let go of your fears and let the light in! Live with the radiance of Christ as you let go and see the brilliance of the Lord shine in you!

Dear Lord,

I will let go of my worries and let You take them all. You promise to calm my heart and soul when I trust You more. There is no room for fear when You are near to me! My worry disappears as I lean on You. I know that You will lighten my load as I let Your light shine down on me. I will cling to the hope in Psalm 34:5, *"Those who look to him are radiant, and their faces shall never be ashamed."*

In Jesus' Name, Amen

April 24

Are You Waiting Patiently for the Lord as you Pray?

The Lord hears us when we cry out to Him. He knows what we need even before we ask Him. He wants us to wait patiently upon Him so that He can answer in *His* timing. He is ready to bless us. He hears every prayer and every thought that enters our minds. He listens to our requests and gives us what we need just when we need it. We learn to trust Him more each day. Spend time in prayer and wait upon the Lord to answer each prayer!

Dear Lord,

You are a comfort to me as I pray. I can feel Your loving arms wrapped around me. I will not give up but will keep praying patiently and fervently for what is on my heart. I know Your timing is perfect and that You hear me as I lift my requests. I will not give up but will wait patiently upon You! I believe Psalm 40:1 and will do the same as I pray, *"I waited patiently for the LORD, he inclined to me and heard my cry."*

In Jesus' Name, Amen

April 25

Do You Believe God is Able?

Are you tired of waiting for answers from the Lord? Have you been praying for what seems like a thousand years? Is your heart heavy with burdens instead of blessings? Remember that a thousand years to you is like a day to the Lord. His timing is perfect for you. He is waiting for you to open your heart and believe. He is wanting you to focus on what you hope for through faith. Your God is able! Give Him praise before you see your answer!

Dear Lord,

Each day is another wonderful opportunity to praise You for who You are! As I trust You more each day, You will show me the way to go. I never have to fear when You are here for me! I believe I will receive all You desire for me. I will keep trusting You! I will wait upon You, because I know that I will see Your promises come to my life! I believe Your promise to me in 2 Peter 3:8, *"With the Lord one day is as a thousand years, and a thousand years as one day."*

In Jesus' Name, Amen

April 26

Are You Pressing into Hope?

Have you lost your hope? Is your heart heavy with burdens and stress? Are you struggling with past mistakes and afraid to step into your future? Turn to Jesus Christ and find your hope in Him! He is right there waiting to take all your hopelessness and turn it into hope again. You have lost your spark because you are looking at your problems and not to God. Fix your eyes on Jesus, the joy of your salvation, and watch the hope rise inside you again! With the Lord, there is always hope! Keep believing and keep praying!

Dear Lord,

Oh, how I thank You for giving me hope as I trust in You. I praise You, Lord, for speaking life into me. I will not let fear set in but will cling to the hope that comes from You, my Savior forever! I know that when I face trouble, You will deliver me as I put my faith in You. You have given me true hope! I will live in hope as I pray Psalm 43:5, *"Hope in God; for I shall again praise him, my salvation and my God."*

In Jesus' Name, Amen

April 27

Are You Finding Your Refuge in God?

Are you struggling with deep pain and heartache from troubles that surround you? Have you lost your hope and strength? In this troubled and uncertain world, there is a *present* help. Your help is found in the arms of Jesus Christ who came to restore and redeem you! He is your true anchor of hope and firm foundation in the storms you face. He sees your pain and weeps with you as your heart hurts. Trust Him to restore your joy once again when He heals you. Let Him comfort you and give you rest.

Dear Lord,

As trouble comes, I know I have a place of refuge in Your loving arms. You wrap me up and keep me safe as I trust You. I will not face my problems alone. You are always present with me! I can count on Your love and comfort because You love and have compassion for all. In this present trouble, I will trust You! I will pray and believe Psalm 46:1, *"God is our refuge and strength, a very present help in trouble."*

In Jesus' Name, Amen

April 28

Why Do You Have Hope?

Have you shared with others the hope that is within you? Do you believe that God is working in your life in a real way? Open your heart and let God in. He will be your guide as you follow Him to freedom. He loves you and desires that you put your security in Him. Be sure of whom you serve and worship the Lord with all that is within you. Tell of His greatness and live out your faith so that others may give God the glory. The next generation needs to see you living out what you believe!

Dear Lord,

You have given me a directive to tell others about You! When I keep silent, I cannot share the hope that is within me. When I speak out without fear about who You are, people will find You and know You. You get all the glory! Hope has a name, and His name is Jesus! *"But in your hearts honor Christ the Lord as holy, always being prepared to make a defense to anyone who asks you for a reason for the hope that is in you; yet do it with gentleness and respect,"* 1 Peter 3:15.

In Jesus' Name, Amen

April 29

Are You Seeking God?

Where are you searching for love? Have you given the Lord all your heart? Or have you lost your desire to run to God? God loves you and is seeking you. He knows your heart and wants to be the King of your heart. He needs you to be still and *know* that He is God. As you yield and let Him in, you will know His great love. He wants you to make Him the love of your life. When you seek after Him, you will find Him. He is waiting for you to seek after Him!

Dear Lord,

I am basking in the glory of Your love for me! It is so good to know that Your love for me is eternal! Your love is constant and never dies. You yearn for me to make the decision to give You all my heart. As I pray Psalm 53:2, I will let these words open my heart, *"God looks down from heaven on the children of man to see if there are any who understand, who seek after God."*

In Jesus' Name, Amen

April 30

Are You Casting Your Burdens on the Lord?

We all have burdens on our hearts that we are carrying. There are many problems that come our way that weigh us down. The Lord will take all our burdens when we give them to Him. He will take the weight that we are carrying and hold all of it for us. Instead of holding onto them, let us cast our cares on our Lord who will carry our burdens. Nothing is too big for Him! Let go and give it all to the Lord so He can give us the freedom we desire!

Dear Lord,

I have come to You asking for Your help to lighten my load. I have been carrying burdens You want me to release to You. In Your perfect timing, I will see what You want to show me. I will let go of fear and let my faith rise. My freedom from the worries I have been carrying is immediate when I release them to You. You sustain me as I cast my burdens to You! I will cling to Your Word in Psalm 55:22, *"Cast your burden on the LORD, and he will sustain you…"*

In Jesus' Name, Amen

Monthly Reflections

As you pray and lean on the Lord's promises, write
what the Lord has revealed to you for this month.

AND LET THE
peace of Christ
rule in your hearts,
to which indeed
YOU WERE CALLED
in one body.
And
be thankful
COLOSSIANS 3:15

May 1

Are You Praising God for His Glory?

Are you praising God for your many blessings? Have you given Him praise for bringing you life? Your life is evidence of His love. God's glory shines down on you to encourage and enrich your life. Only the Lord can fully strengthen you for what you are facing. Add God to your challenge and watch Him do the impossible for you. You will strengthen one day at a time when you faithfully walk one step at a time. Humble yourself before God and He will exalt you at the proper time. Keep your faith and walk obediently with the Lord who wants to be with You every moment of your journey!

Dear Lord,

Thank You for touching my heart again and again as I praise You in my prayers. I am basking in great joy as the Holy Spirit is active and alive in me. I am praising You for Your glory all around me! Thank You for giving me new hope as I see Your radiant light! *"Be exalted, O God, above the heavens! Let your glory be over all the earth*!" Psalm 57:11.

In Jesus' Name, Amen

May 2

Are You Lonely?

The Lord wants to replace your loneliness with joy. He will wait with you as you patiently wait upon Him. As you wait in silence for your Lord, your soul will be renewed and replenished with a fullness of joy! As you find joy, your loneliness disappears! Your despair turns into delight as you wait upon the Lord instead of worrying about being alone. You are not alone. Take heart, the Lord is your constant companion and will bring you peace and joy to rejuvenate your lonely heart!

Dear Lord,

I am not alone when You are Lord of my life. You promise to never leave or forsake me. Your love never ends! I am Yours and You are mine. I have made You the Keeper of my soul. I know that even when I am by myself, I will always have You with me. I can talk to You and walk with You whenever I choose. You are waiting patiently for me to pray and live out my faith one step at a time. Psalm 62:1 refreshes my soul as I pray, *"For God alone my soul waits in silence; from him comes my salvation."*

In Jesus' Name, Amen

May 3

Are You Stepping into Your Destiny?

Are you letting your fears prevent you from walking through the door set before you? Do you know your God-made plan has been laid out before you? God has opened a door for you that no man can shut. Step into the destiny that God has planned for you. Walk through the door! Let your faith rise and your fear fade as you trust God to walk with you. Be confident as you obey His will for you! You are secure in Christ, your way-maker! Let Him show you the way to freedom!

Dear Lord,

Thank You for setting an open door before me that no one can shut! I will walk in the way You want me to go even when it seems impossible. Because I *know* that nothing is impossible with You! I will trust You to show me the way as I pray for direction. Instead of letting fear set in, I will walk faithfully and confidently with You. Lead me, Lord, through that open door. I believe Your promise to me in Revelation 3:8, *"Behold, I have set before you an open door, which no one is able to shut."*

In Jesus' Name, Amen

May 4

Do You See the Open Door?

Sometimes we have an open door set before us, but we fail to see it. God wants us to walk in a specific direction, but we lack the confidence to move forward. Instead of looking to God, we let fear and doubt settle in us. We serve a mighty God who is bigger than any problem we might face! If He opens a door for us, no one will be able to shut it! Be encouraged with Christ and press on to victory through the door set before us! *"For a wide door for effective work has opened to me, and there are many adversaries,"* 1 Corinthians 16:9.

Dear Lord,

I see the open door and I will walk through it no matter who tries to come against me. I hear You telling me that I can work for You if I let You lead me through the door. I am encouraged to know You are *for* me and not against me! There is nothing man can do to me!

In Jesus Name, Amen

May 5

Are You Mourning a Loss?

Are you mourning a loss in your life? Is your heart broken and your body weary? Come to the Lord when you are heavy ladened and burdened and He will give you comfort and rest. He will fill the empty places of your heart and soul with His love and joy. He will give you His perfect peace. You can rest knowing He will bless you in amazing ways when you trust Him. Let go and let the Lord help you. He will bind up your wounds and heal you.

Dear Lord,

When I weep, You weep with me. I know I am blessed even when I mourn because You are with me. In the darkest moments, You bring the greatest light! I find my strength and comfort from You as I trust You. I want You to fill the pain with promise. I love You and believe You are with me in these hard times. I will embrace Your love and find refuge in Your arms. *"Blessed are those who mourn, for they shall be comforted,"* Matthew 5:4.

In Jesus' Name, Amen

May 6

Why Are You So Anxious?

Are you worried today? Have you let anxiety take hold of you to the point of panic? Are you burdened and afraid of things you cannot change? Be still and let the peace of Christ enter your soul. He wants to take your concerns and turn them to hope once again. You are stronger with the Lord than you have ever been! He will be your strength for this mountain you are facing. Keep pressing on to victory and let the peace of Christ rule in you as you go!

Dear Lord,

I have been afraid of what might happen which leads to anxiety and fear. Instead of letting Your peace rule in my heart, I have been wrestling with my anxious thoughts. O Lord, calm my anxious heart and still my soul with Your peace. I will choose peace instead of fear. I will bring all my worries to You, one at a time. It is well with my soul. You are the center of my life. Matthew 6:27 reminds me to let go of worry as I read, *"And which of you by being anxious can add a single hour to his span of life?"*

In Jesus' Name, Amen

May 7

Are You Looking to God in the Face of Trouble?

Are you trusting God with all that you are facing now? Do your problems seem insurmountable? Look to the Lord for all that you need. He is a present help for you! He is there for you right here, right now. He wants to take your sins away and wash you with the blood of Jesus. Focus on God and not your troubles. Look up and let Him shine His face upon you! Your troubles will fade, and your life will be made new as you fix your eyes on Jesus Christ!

Dear Lord,

In the midst of chaos and confusion, You are there for me. In the uncertainty that each day brings, You are my certainty. In the insecurity of this world, You are my security. In the pain and pressure, You are my peace. In the instability, You are my stability. In the darkness, You are my light! In the suffering, You are my joy! *"May God be gracious to us and bless us and make his face to shine upon us,"* Psalm 67:1.

In Jesus' Name, Amen

May 8

Is Your Worry Winning?

Have you let your worries win? Is your stress too much to bear? Take it all to the Lord and let Him wash you with His peace. Peace will flood your heart when you ponder your abundant blessings. Your restlessness will turn to fear if you let it. Instead of worrying about what might happen, thank God for His saving grace and abundant love for you. Instead of being depressed and dejected, thank God for what He has done for you. His love for you is real and never ending! Let your mouth be filled with His praise!

Dear Lord,

Thank You for loving me! I am so grateful for Your love that never ends and Your grace that forever saves! I will step out of myself and listen to what You are telling me. Your love has opened the door to blessings in my life! My perspective has changed since I have yielded to You! The Holy Spirit fills me with joy and peace that no one can take away! No challenge can take away my hope! *"My mouth is filled with your praise, and with your glory all the day,"* Psalm 71:8.

In Jesus' Name, Amen

May 9

How Can We Have Peace When There is so
Much Stress Around Us?

Have you turned away from the peace of
Christ because of your fear and anxiety? Are your
burdens too much to bear because you are stressed
and worried? Be still and let the peace of Christ fill
your soul again. Abide in the love of Jesus by letting
go of all your fears and clinging to the vine of life!
Jesus is the vine, and we are the branches. When we
draw our nourishment from the Spirit in the vine, we
can produce good fruit that remains. Let the Spirit, as
power from the vine, nourish you to new life today!

Dear Lord,

I will abide in You to know Your perfect
peace that remains even in the face of trouble. I have
seen You change my fear of the unknown into peace.
I will abide in You. My stress disappears when I cling
to Your Spirit for strength and endurance. I believe
the promise in John 15:4, *"Abide in me, and I in you.
As the branch cannot bear fruit by itself, unless it
abides in the vine, neither can you, unless you abide
in me."*

In Jesus' Name, Amen

May 10

Are You Longing for Joy?

Are you looking for joy where there is only heartache and brokenness? Do you need a friend who can help and encourage you? Ask Jesus to live inside you and discover pure joy that is real. In His presence, there is fullness of joy! In His arms, all your fears will subside and turn to joy! You need to be encouraged and strengthened for what you will face. The problems are real, and the pain is sure to come, but with Jesus, you can still have joy through it all! Grab tight to Jesus and see that all is well with your soul!

Dear Lord,

I have joy only because You live inside me. I know the fullness of joy because I know You as my Lord and Savior. In Your presence is fullness of joy and at Your right hand are pleasures forevermore. I will keep praying for all to believe in You so that all can know the power of Your love and fullness of Your joy! *"Until now you have asked nothing in my name. Ask, and you shall receive, that your joy may be full,"* John 16:24.

In Jesus' Name, Amen

May 11

Do You Believe God Can Use You?

God has begun a good work in us and needs us to complete His work. He is ready for us to stand firm and stand up to what we have been called to do. It is time to put aside our fears and let Him work through us. If we are willing, He will use our gifts and talents for His glory! It is not time to isolate ourselves from God, but time to reach out to God so that He can build us up for the work He has begun and will finish in us. We all have a purpose and God needs us to begin it now!

Dear Lord,

As I pray today, Your joy floods my heart! It seems unreal to have such joy in these times of uncertainty, but You have pulled me closer to Your love during this time. I will finish the work You have started in me! Philippians 1:6 gives me hope as I pray today. *"And I am sure of this, that he who began a good work in you will bring it to completion at the day of Jesus Christ."*

In Jesus' Name, Amen

May 12

Did You Know You Have an Inheritance in the Lord?

When we believe in the Lord Jesus Christ, we have our inheritance in Him. We are His children, heirs of God, when we choose to believe. We can be sure of His love for us which never ends and never changes! Jesus is the same yesterday, today, and forever! Our lives are in His hands when we trust Him. As we take His hand, we are living by faith and acting in faith with our Lord. He is our true King who has given us an inheritance in Him!

Dear Lord,

Thank You for giving me rest. I have found comfort in Your arms. I know Your hand is upon me. I will find comfort in knowing I have my inheritance in You. I am sure of Your love for me! I will let go of fear and let You build my faith! I will cling to You and Your promises to me! I believe Ephesians 1:11, *"In him we have obtained an inheritance…"*

In Jesus' Name, Amen

May 13

Do You Want to be Restored?

Do you yearn to come back to your place of joy? Is your heart calling you to believe again or for the first time? Draw closer to the Lord so He can draw closer to you! He wants to restore you to the joy of your salvation! He sees your struggle and knows your heart. He loves every part of you and wants to see you happy again. There is so much heartache all around us but there is always joy in Jesus Christ! Take His hand and let Him bring You closer to His heart! He is calling you closer! Do you hear Him?

Dear Lord,

Thank You for restoring the joy of my salvation as I have drawn closer to You! You are the one who will lead me wherever I need to go. You lead me through the fire and through the storms. I know Your hand of protection is guiding me safely. I have joy in all circumstances because of Your love for me. I am sure of Your steadfast love for me! I pray Psalm 85:4 for all, *"Restore us again, O God of our salvation…"*

In Jesus' name, Amen

May 14

Have You Received Grace to Give Grace?

Have you accepted love and forgiveness from Jesus Christ? Is your heart turned toward the one who has taken all your sins and forgiven you? Take His hand and walk in forgiveness and forgive those who need you to forgive them. When you are tenderhearted and kind, you are giving grace and love to those in need. Give grace as grace has been given to you. Come to the cross where grace reigns and lay down all your cares and worries at the feet of Jesus who will take them all!

Dear Lord,

You have brought me grace upon grace through Your sacrifice. I am healed because I have come to You! I can rest knowing that I am forgiven. I am free to love and extend grace to those around me. It is well with my soul now that I have You in my heart. Because I have made my home with You, I can forgive those who have hurt me and be kind and tenderhearted to all. *"Be kind to one another, tenderhearted, forgiving one another, as God in Christ forgave you*," Ephesians 4:32.

In Jesus' Name, Amen

May 15

Are You Awake?

Are you feeling lifeless and spiritually dead? Has your hope disappeared because of what you see around you? Are you unsure of where to turn? Wake up to new life with Jesus Christ! He is waiting to usher in new hope for you! Even in this battle, He is right there holding you up. Rise up to victory with the one who carries your burdens. Give Him your heart and come alive on the inside to experience His living hope that never ceases. He will turn your boredom to bravery and your depression to delight so that you can see His light!

Dear Lord,

Thank You for shining Your light upon me as I stay awake with You. I know You are real and so powerful. There is nothing that You cannot do! I am trusting You right now in this storm around me. You bring good out of the pain and hope from heartache. I pray for all to wake up and touch You, Lord. You are waiting for each of us as Ephesians 5:14 so beautifully promises, *"Awake, O sleeper, and arise from the dead, and Christ will shine on you."*

In Jesus' Name, Amen

May 16

Do You Know the Lord Has His Angels Guarding You?

We can feel secure in the truth that we have angels around us guarding us in this storm we are facing. Even when we are afraid, God's angels are all around us protecting us from harm. The Lord has His army of angels in place to guard us. God is ever present with us! When we call on Him, He will be there for us. God commands His angels over us and will fight our battle. Take heart and be confident of the victory that is ours through Jesus Christ!

Dear Lord,

I have placed my trust and security in You to bring me through this storm. It is surreal what I am facing today, but with You, there is greater hope! I will keep believing for greater miracles with greater faith. I am praying for all to take this time to grow closer to You! It is through the struggles that we see Your glory shining the brightest! I believe You are doing greater things through these challenging times! *"For he will command his angels concerning you to guard you in all your ways,"* Psalm 91:11.

In Jesus' Name, Amen

May 17

Do You Need to be Rescued?

Are you feeling weak? Have you given up because the battle is waging inside you? Draw strength and courage from God. He will give you all you need to face your giant. He hears your cries for help as you pray, and He will comfort you. Be brave because you are about to see victory. Keep trusting and obeying. It is not time to quit, but it is time to shine as the light of Christ shines in you! Keep going with the strong hand of God upon you! Why are you so afraid? Impossible is where our God begins!

Dear Lord,

Oh, how I need Your strength! I know that you will fulfill all my needs and make me strong and brave. You promise to be with me when I let you in. Help me, Lord, as I believe in Your promises. As I let go of my fear and trust, You will deliver me. Oh, how I love to read Your truth in Psalm 82:4, *"Rescue the weak and needy; deliver them from the hand of the wicked."*

In Jesus' name, Amen

May 18

Is Your Heart Open to Pray for Others to Find Christ?

We live in communities with multiple opportunities for connection. We can encourage others as we reach out in love and pray for each other. Our prayers bring hope. Our testimonies of faith lift spirits. Sharing the Word strengthens souls. People need to know God is real. When we love others with the love of Christ, they see His love in action. God wants us to pray for each other and work together to build up each other's faith. Let's make the heart connection by bringing others to God in prayer.

Dear Lord,

I know there are people who do not know You. There is much work to do for You. You have been waiting for Your children to come to You. May we all share our hearts together as we connect to You with our prayers. *"Complete my joy by being of the same mind, having the same love, being in full accord and of one mind," Philippians 2:2.*

In Jesus' Name, Amen

May 19

Are You Still Rejoicing?

Will you rejoice in the Lord even during pain? Have you come closer to His heart even when your heart aches? Is your hope found in the light of Jesus Christ? Find hope through Jesus Christ even in these concerning and uncertain times! Rejoice in the Lord for all His goodness and grace! Let His love enrich your life moment by moment. Continue praising even in the fear. Keep praying even in the pain. Remain hopeful even if you cannot understand. Stay faithful for when the test comes. Keep drawing to His Word of life. Keep fighting the good fight of the faith!

Dear Lord,

I will not let go of my faith even in these challenging times! You are with me always, no matter what I face. I will keep worshipping and praising You even in the storm! I will trust You even if I do not understand. I will spread the good news of Your love available for everyone to receive. I will keep praying for all to be made spiritually and physically well! And I will rejoice as Philippians 3:1 encourages me, *"Rejoice in the Lord..."*

In Jesus' Name, Amen

May 20

Are You Strong in the Lord?

Are you fixing your eyes on the problem or the solution? Is your mind heavy with anxious thoughts about tomorrow? Have you asked Jesus for new strength? Press into the total power of the Lord and relinquish your fear. He wants to be your lifeline of faith in these unpredictable times. Make His word your anchor and hold on tight to His promises! He will put His Spirit inside you to guide you in the days ahead. Do not worry. Wait upon the Lord! He will strengthen you for every challenge that comes your way!

Dear Lord,

O, how I thank You for Your promise to never leave or forsake me! You will give me new strength when I trust you to help me. Even at my weakest, I feel Your power come alive inside of me because I believe Philippians 4:13, *"I can do all things through him who strengthens me."*

In Jesus' Name, Amen

May 21

Are You Finding Life in Jesus?

God made us in His image to be loved. He wants us to know Him and to abide. We are His sheep in need of a Good Shepherd to lead us. When we need guidance, He is there. When we are lost, He will save us. When we need hope, He will rescue us! When we need strength, He will empower us. When we need peace, He will comfort us. When we are lost, He will find us! *"Whoever finds his life will lose it, and whoever loses his life for my sake will find it,"* Matthew 10:39.

Dear Lord,

I know that You want me to make sacrifices to follow You. If I lose my life for You, I will certainly find it! I will follow You to freedom and joy as I hear You speaking hope to me. I will keep letting You work in me, my Lord. You give me new life.

In Jesus' Name, Amen

May 22

Do You Know that God is Your Good Shepherd?

Are you needing to be rescued from this world? Is your heart heavy with burdens you cannot handle right now? Take heart, and let God show you the way. He made you with the need to be protected and strengthened. He needs you to know you are not alone. He knows your heart and wants to help you. Know He is with you wherever you go. Lay down in His green pastures, beside still waters, and you will find rest for your soul!

Dear Lord,

Thank You for rescuing me when I was lost. You have forgiven me and have saved my soul from death. You love me with an everlasting love that enriches my life and brings joy to my heart! I am at peace knowing You will guide and protect me. Psalm 100:3 blesses my soul as I read, *"Know that the LORD, he is God! It is he who made us, and we are his; we are his people, and the sheep of his pasture."* I am Yours and am blessed by You, my Good Shepherd!

In Jesus' Name, Amen

May 23

Where is Your Peace Found?

We all strive for peace in a world where things are constantly changing. When the peace of Christ rules in our hearts, we will find His perfect peace no matter what is happening around us. Only Jesus brings peace that lasts forever. He gives us this great gift when we trust Him with all our hearts. There can be unrest and chaos around us, but when we have the peace of Christ, we are free, indeed! Yes, the peace of Christ will fill us with security and freedom! Choose His peace that passes all understanding and be set free!

Dear Lord,

I am at peace because I know You as my Lord and Savior. Only You can bring me the perfect peace that restores my soul. In this world where fear reigns, I will choose peace. Only Your peace will help me. My soul is free as I turn everything over to you! Thank you for giving me peace! Even in the storm, I am praising You for my peace as I read Mark 4:39, *"Peace, be still!"*

In Jesus' Name, Amen

May 24

Are You Continuing to Pray?

God wants us to pray steadfastly for what is on our heart. He knows our needs and our hearts' desires. He wants to answer the cries of our hearts, but we must take them to the Lord in prayer. When we just keep them to ourselves, we miss out on the opportunity for His blessing and fellowship. God loves to hear us pray. He wants to give us the desires of our hearts as we delight in Him! Keep praying and be watchful for how and when God answers!

Dear Lord,

Oh, how I love to pray to You! I know without a doubt that You will answer me! I know You want me to set my heart on You so You can show me what the desires you have for me. My relationship with You has grown as I have continued praying and reading Your Word of truth. Your Word encourages my soul. I will listen to You as I pray and obey Your Word as Colossians 4:2 reminds me, *"Continue steadfastly in prayer, being watchful in it with thanksgiving."*

In Jesus' Name, Amen

May 25

Are You Living What You Believe?

God knows our hearts and He sees our actions. He wants us to keep pleasing Him with how we live. Our faith is lived out by how we treat others. Are we walking in a way that is honoring God? Have we put feet to our faith? People need Jesus and we might be the one person who shows faith in action through our kindness and compassion. Be the hands and feet of Jesus by loving others like Jesus loves! One act of kindness can revive hearts and restore souls!

Dear Lord,

You are so real to me and such a wonderful example for me to follow. I thank You for the opportunities to share Your love with those around me. I can hear You guiding me to act in ways that will please You. Your Living Word gives me hope. Even when my problems seem impossible and insurmountable, Your presence brings joy and peace to my soul! I will act in ways that please You, Lord, each and every day! *"Please God, just as you are doing, that you do so more and more,"* 1 Thessalonians 4:1.

In Jesus' Name, Amen

May 26

Do You See the Great Works
of the Lord Around You?

The Lord has done great things for us to see. Bask in His majesty and glory surrounding us! As we look around us, we can see wonders of His handiwork. His hands are upon us as we come to Him. We can rest knowing He has the whole world in His hands. As we reach out to God, we will experience His mercy and grace upon us. He loves us with an everlasting love. Experience His love and grace and let the peace of Christ come alive in your heart!

Dear Lord,

I am delighting in Your love as I let the Holy Spirit guide me into all truth. I see the wonder of Your love all around me, Lord. Thank You for creating new life within me so that I can face these uncertain times. As I focus on You, I see glimpses of Your glory all around me! I am praising You for creating me with eyes to see Your majesty and beauty! *"Great are the works of the LORD, studied by all who delight in them,"* Psalm 111:2.

In Jesus' Name, Amen

May 27

Do You Believe that God Will Strengthen You?

God hears our prayers. He helps the afflicted in body, mind, and spirit. He heals our hearts when we come to Him and bring our requests to Him. We are not perfect, and we certainly make mistakes, but God is sure to save us when we surrender all to Him. He hears us immediately and strengthens us as we lay all our burdens down at His feet. Lay it all down and receive His mercy and grace.

Dear Lord,

Thank You for hearing the cry of my heart. You know my weaknesses and struggles and will incline Your ear to my prayers. I am sorry for letting the stress around me take over my actions. I will supplement my faith with virtue, self-control, brotherly love, godliness, and steadfastness even in the hardest of times. Because I know You love me eternally, I will pray believing the promises in Psalm 10:17, "*O LORD, you hear the desire of the afflicted; you will strengthen their heart; you will incline your ear.*"

In Jesus' Name, Amen

May 28

Why Are You Afraid of the Bad News?

Are you clinging to the hope of Christ or to the insurmountable problems you are facing? Is fear stealing your joy or is the good news of Christ settling in your heart to bring you peace? You can have all the hope, joy, and peace you need when you trust the Lord. He is real to those who put Him in the center of their lives. Let go of the worry and invite the Lord in the places of your heart that need revival and restoration. Beloved, He loves you so much and longs to be the love of your life!

Dear Lord,

Oh, how I need You! I am praying for more of Your love, hope, joy, and peace. Take away the pain and pressures I am facing and restore to me the joy of my salvation so that I can be revived again! I believe in You and will worship You and not the temporal things of this world! Your Word is true and real for me today, and it comforts me. *"He is not afraid of bad news; his heart is firm, trusting in the LORD,"* Psalm 112:7.

In Jesus' Name, Amen

May 29

What is Your Aim?

Are you loving others from a pure heart that loves unconditionally? Does your love flow from a sincere faith and a good conscience because you are close to God? Keep loving God and give your love to others. God knows your heart like no one else. He loves you and wants a deeper relationship with you. Set your heart on God and see His love come to life in you! His love will conquer all!

Dear Lord,

I pray that my aim in this world will be to love more. Even when I do not understand, help me to love You. Help me rise to victory so that I can freely live! I pray that everyone will come together as one heart and soul to pray for healing and restoration for all. No matter where we are, we can *pray*! It is so good to be able to pray together in one accord with one heart and soul. Today as I pray let me remember my charge from 1 Timothy 1:5, *"The aim of our charge is love that issues from a pure heart and a good conscience and a sincere faith."*

In Jesus' Name, Amen

May 30

Do You See God's Majesty During Uncertain Times?

God is real. He loves us and is certainly there for us. He gives us glimpses of His power as He shows His majesty and wonder in the heavens above! He has made heaven and earth and all that is with it. He wants to remind us that He is in control and will make all things beautiful in its time. We must trust Him to see His plan unfold for us. Trust first, and then He will show us the way! Psalm 115:3 reminds us that, *"Our God is in the heavens; he does all that he pleases."*

Dear Lord,

I believe in You and have Your peace even in these uncertain times. As I trust and follow You, I have let go of my old self and have been created new in You through Your power that lives inside me. As I pray today, I thank you for Your majesty in the heavens! I will press into Your love as I let the Holy Spirit lead me. I have received the power of the Holy Spirit and I am at peace.

In Jesus' Name, Amen

May 31

Do You Believe that
God Answers Your Prayers?

Are you worrying or praying? God wants you to turn your worry list into a prayer list. Do you believe that God will answer your prayers or are you afraid that He will not answer you? God always hears your prayers and has an answer for each one. The answers are all in His timing and His will. God's answer will come as you keep praying and believing. He is listening to you as you talk to Him. He knows your heart and wants to bless you, His beloved! Keep your faith and continue praying from your heart!

Dear Lord,

I am comforted as I call to You and read Your Word, my Lord! My faith has grown stronger with each Word I read and each prayer I pray. You have answered so many prayers and I am humbled and grateful for each one. Your peace flows like a fountain overflowing in my soul as I pray and read Your Word. Psalm 116:2 captures the essence of my devotion to You, *"Because he inclined his ear to me, therefore I will call on him as long as I live."*

In Jesus' Name, Amen

Monthly Reflections

As you pray and lean on the Lord's promises, write
what the Lord has revealed to you for this month.

TRUST IN THE LORD
with all your
HEART,
and do not lean
on your own
UNDERSTANDING.
PROVERBS 3:5

June 1

Are You Staying Faithful?

Not all have faith, but the Lord is faithful *all* the time. He wants us to keep our faith even when life seems impossible. With God, *all* things are possible! Just when we think the battle is beyond our control, God reminds us that *He* is in control. He will fight our battles when we keep our faith. Letting go and letting Him step in takes faith. Our faith will grow as we step out of our comfort zones and put our faith first!

Dear Lord,

It is impossible to be strong without You. I cannot finish my race if I take my eyes off You. In this world where there is still sin, I need to draw closer to You by faith. Impossible is where You begin! I believe You will answer the prayers of your people who humble themselves and pray to be free of the sin that so easily entangles us. As we all turn from our old ways and turn to You, our living hope, we will see healing and wholeness as we are made new in You! *"Fight the good fight of the faith…"* 1 Timothy 6:12.

In Jesus' Name, Amen

June 2

Are You Living by the Example of Jesus?

Are you following the light of Christ who brings love? Is your hope found in Jesus? He will forgive you. Your Savior has come to bring you hope in the valleys. He will help you with whatever you are facing today and what you will face in the future. Trust Him to help you through this dark time. Give Jesus your heart and be set free from the things that are holding you captive to sin!

Dear Lord,

In these times of unrest, let me live by the example of our Savior, Jesus Christ. Jesus walked on this earth as man and experienced even darker times. He knew that He must draw closer to You, Father God, to find peace, so He prayed. He prayed and found comfort and hope. He prayed and heard You speak truth and life to Him. He knew what He must do and did it. He never stopped praying! Let me follow the example of Jesus and stay faithful to You, my Lord, who is always faithful to me! *"Follow the pattern of the sound words that you have heard from me, in the faith and the love that are in Christ Jesus,"* 2 Timothy 1:13.

In Jesus' Name, Amen

June 3

Are You Ready for Your Best Days Ahead?

When we focus on Jesus and fix our eyes upon Him, we will see great and mighty things He wants to show us. He has a purpose He needs us to fulfill. Sometimes we need to let go of something or someone that is holding us back from our God-given destiny. The former things will disappear as we press on to our new, Christ-centered life!

Dear Lord,

My faith in You has given me hope even in the toughest times. I believe You will make all things new, so I will let go of former things that have kept my focus off You. My eyes are fixed on You, Lord, the perfecter of my faith and lover of my soul. I will press on by faith as I open the eyes of my heart to see You. Thank You for showing me the way to new life as I let go and feel Your glorious presence awakening me! *"Behold, the former things have come to pass, and the new things I now declare; before they spring forth, I tell you of them,"* Isaiah 42:9.

In Jesus' Name, Amen

June 4

Are You Pursuing Peace and Love?

Peace and love are still possible through Jesus Christ no matter what we face in this world. The world tells us to put our own interests first, while Jesus tells us to love the Lord first and put others before ourselves. The peace and love of Christ will rule in our hearts when we let Him reign over our thoughts and actions. Jesus wants us to be faithful to Him by living in a way that pleases Him. Righteous living is not a burden, but a blessing! It is more blessed to give than to receive!

Dear Lord,

I know You are the way to peace, love, righteousness, and faith. When I pursue You with a pure heart, I will see all these qualities come to life in me. As I let go of self and former ways of living, I will be made new in You! I am praying for more of You and less of me. I pray for peace and love to reign with righteousness inside of me! *"So flee youthful passion and pursue righteousness, faith, love, and peace along with those who call on the Lord from a pure heart,"* 2 Timothy 2:22.

In Jesus' Name, Amen

June 5

Are You Feeling Weak and Weary?

Are you about to give up because you do not see a way out? Is your faith faltering because you are weary? Let the Lord strengthen you for the rest of the journey. He has called you and set you apart for greater purposes that you have not even seen yet. If you give up, you will not see all that has been promised for you and for those who you have been praying for. Set your heart on Jesus, and your mind on the things above, and you will discover a courage like never before!

Dear Lord,

I come to You today with so much on my mind. The pressures and problems around me are overwhelming at times. But I know You can move mountains in front of me like You have done before. You need me to stand by You and allow You to strengthen me for all my decisions and challenges. I am stronger and braver when I surrender to You. *"But the Lord stood by me and strengthened me..."* 2 Timothy 4:17.

In Jesus' Name, Amen

June 6

Is the Word of God Alive in You?

Is your Bible open or closed? Have you looked for wisdom from above as you pray? Are you listening to God for direction? God is always there for you. No matter what time it is, you can call upon the Lord and He will be there for you! Open your Bible and read what He is telling you to do. The answers are not far away. As you pray to Him, you will indeed grow closer to His love. Hear Him calling you into a deeper relationship with Him by putting His Word into action!

Dear Lord,

You want to have a deeper relationship me. As I let the Holy Spirit guide me into all truth, I am being a doer of Your Holy Word. I will be Spirit-led so You can show me what to do. I will follow You each step of my journey. Holy Spirit, lead me into all truth as I pray today! My breakthrough is coming as I let Your presence be my open door! *"But be doers of the word, and not hearers only, deceiving yourselves,"* James 1:22.

In Jesus' Name, Amen

June 7

Are You Walking in the
Power of God's Love?

Is your heart purposed to love and forgive? Have you been fearing the Lord by listening to Him as you come back to your first love? The Lord Jesus Christ has forgiven you. He wants you to come back to Him by giving Him your whole heart. He knows your deepest desires, and your challenges, and wants to help you. He wants a relationship with you because He loves you, His beloved. Make Him the Lord of your life so you can live with the power of *His* love in you!

Dear Lord,

By Your grace I have been saved. By Your love I am set free! I want to have a deeper relationship with You, Lord! As I pray, I am listening to You speak to me in love. My heart is rejoicing as I let go and let You show me the way. In Your love, I will find everything I need! Be still my soul. *"Blessed is everyone who fears the LORD, who walks in his ways!"* Psalm 128:1.

In Jesus' Name, Amen

June 8

Do You Know the Risen Jesus?

Jesus died for us so that we could live forgiven and free! When we invite Him in our hearts, He lives in us. He wants us to know Him. Invite the Savior of the world to live in your heart. He has risen, indeed! When we know the Risen Jesus, we will have peace. He gives us the Holy Spirit who is Jesus in us. Receive the Holy Spirit and know His peace that passes all understanding! He has risen, indeed!

Dear Lord,

I am rejoicing with great joy as I ponder Your glory in my life! I know You live in my heart and soul. I am thankful I have a real relationship with You, my Lord and Savior. The Holy Spirit is active and alive within me. I am praising You, Lord, for the joy of my salvation! Thank You for saving me so that I can live eternally with You. I love You! *"He has risen; he is not here…"* Mark 16:6.

In Jesus' Name, Amen

June 9

Have You Opened Your Bible to Find Your Answers?

The Word of the Lord remains forever. He has given us His Word so we can learn and know the truth. All the answers are in the Bible. When we open its pages and let the words come alive in us, we find the truth. God wants us to write His Word on our hearts. A closed Bible will not give us hope. Open your Bible with an open heart and mind, believe what you read, and find the hope that awaits you!

Dear Lord,

Thank You for Your Word that remains forever in my heart. You meet me each day as I open my Bible, and my heart, to Your truth. As I read each page, I believe what You are telling me. Today as I pray, I want to praise You for all that You have been showing me as I read Your Word. I will keep reading and praying to deepen my relationship with You! "*All flesh is like grass and all its glory like the flower of grass. The grass withers, and the flower falls, but the word of the Lord remains foreve*r," 1 Peter 1:24-25.

In Jesus' Name, Amen

June 10

Are You Calling on the Lord
to Increase Your Strength?

When you are weary, where do you turn? God is eager to help you when you need strength. When your heart is broken, where do you seek refuge? God will shelter you in His wings. When you need someone to talk to, who do you turn to? God is patiently waiting for you to talk to Him as you pray. Open your heart, and let the Lord speak to you. He will be your hiding place.

Dear Lord,

Today I pray for strength. With You, I can press on! I am encouraged by what You are speaking to me through Your Word. You have built up my faith and strengthened my soul. I will rely more on You each day. I know You are busy working and building Your Kingdom in heaven for those who believe. I will join in this work here on Earth, helping build your Kingdom. To God the glory! *"On the day I called, you answered me; my strength of soul you increase*d," Psalm 138:3.

In Jesus' Name, Amen

June 11

What Does Waiting on the Lord Mean to You?

Are you waiting on the Lord? Are you trusting the Lord to walk with you? He is *always* with you wherever you go. The world says to rush and receive instant gratification, but God says, "Wait on Me and I will restore you." Waiting takes patience and persistence, and God knows that. He rewards those who walk in His way and keep the faith. A thousand years is like one day to the Lord, so keep praying and working for His timing. The Lord is coming soon, so wait upon Him!

Dear Lord,

You came for me so that I could have a relationship with You now and for eternity! How amazing, Lord! I am blessed by You and Your promises to me. I will keep the faith as I patiently wait on You. You have promised to come again. Until that glorious day, I will fulfill the ministry You have given me with patience and persistence, one day at a time! "*Be patient, therefore, brothers, until the coming of the Lord,*" James 5:7.

In Jesus' Name, Amen

June 12

Have You Lifted Your Worries to the Lord?

Have you lifted your worries as prayers to the Lord and asked Him for wisdom? If you give them to Him, The Lord will take your worries and burdens. Your prayers are sweet like incense rising up to the Father. Are you praying in faith? Believe that God will answer your prayers in His will and timing as you pray. Feel the peace of Christ seep into your soul as you pray. He will strengthen you. Keep praying and do not stop believing! His answers will come as you pray and believe!

Dear Lord,

There are multiple things that could bring me down in this world, but I will not let worry win. I am stronger only because of Your presence in me. As I pray, I feel Your power come alive in my heart and soul. I can breathe because You are in me! There is *power* through the blood of Jesus! Hear my prayers as I lift them all up to You! *"Let my prayer be counted as incense before you, and the lifting up of my hands as the evening sacrifice!"* Psalm 141:2.

In Jesus' Name, Amen

June 13

Are You Seeking the Lord with all Your Heart?

Have you been faithfully following the Lord with all your heart? When you follow Him and put your feet to your faith, you will find your destiny. Is your fear keeping you from being effective? He has been waiting for you to step forth in courage. When you call upon the name of the Lord, He will answer you. When you give Him your whole heart, He will fill your heart and your soul with His Spirit. Keep the faith and listen to Your Lord!

Dear Lord,

There are days when I just do not have the words I want to pray. But I know I all need to do is call upon your name. You know my thoughts and needs from afar before I even speak them. You will rejuvenate me as I spend time with You. Peace will surround me when I release all my worries and let You in. I have found You, Lord, and it is well with my soul! *"You will seek me and find me, when you seek me with all your heart,"* Jeremiah 29:13.

In Jesus' Name, Amen

June 14

Do You Know You Are Fearfully and Wonderfully Made?

God made you in His wonder and glory to be who you are. He magnificently knit you in your mother's womb! He wants you to believe you are loved and worthy in His eyes. He loves *every* part of you, His beloved! Be devoted to the one who loves You bountifully and gives you eternal life. You are specially made by God. Know that you are loved! He specially designed you and made you to be fearless. Take hold of His hand and let Him lead you to your destiny!

Dear Lord,

I know my destiny is in Your hands. I will step out in faith and follow You. In You, my faith will increase daily. I know I am fearfully and wonderfully made and am special in Your eyes. You made me with love to share my faith and Your love with others. I will keep praising You all the days of my life! *"I praise you, for I am fearfully and wonderfully made. Wonderful are your works; my soul knows it very well,"* Psalm139:14.

In Jesus' Name, Amen

June 15

Do You Need Mercy?

Are you seeking comfort and do not know where to turn? The Lord is near and will support you as you seek Him. Is your heart broken and you feel like you have lost your way? Cry out to the Lord who will attend to the voice of your prayer and heal your broken heart. The Guardian of your soul will touch you with His grace and give you mercy. He never waivers and always gives. Ask, and you shall receive mercy so that your joy may be full!

Dear Lord,

I need You more each day to guide and direct me. It is so good to know there is nothing I can do to make You love me less. Even when I mess up, You give me grace and tell me you love me. It is well with my soul! *"With my voice I cry out to the LORD; with my voice, I plead for mercy to the LORD,"* Psalm 142:1.

In Jesus' Name, Amen

June 16

Do You Feel Abandoned?

Do you feel abandoned? The Lord will rescue you when you seek Him. Is your heart restless? Come closer to the love of the Lord and He will comfort you as you lie down in His green pastures. Fear the Lord and know that He wants to help you. Those who seek Him, will find Him. Those who enter through His door, will be safe in the sheepfold of the Good Shepherd, the Keeper of your soul!

Dear Lord,

When I am in Your presence, I am full of life and free of worry. I praise You, for I am fearfully and wonderfully made in Your image! I know Your voice, and I hear You calling me to come closer to You, my Good Shepherd. I am not lost when I stay in Your sheepfold where You fill my soul. It is well with my soul as I rest in Your steadfast love. Thank You for finding me and restoring my soul! *"Behold, the eye of the LORD is on those who fear him, on those who hope in his steadfast love."* Psalm 33:18.

In Jesus' Name, Amen

June 17

What is Your Heart's Desire?

Are you praying for what is on your heart? Have you continued to pray even when you cannot see the details? God loves to hear you pray and will bless you with His peace. Do you believe God will grant you your heart's desire? Keep praying for what is on your heart and believe that God can do what seems impossible! God has the best plan for you, so keep praying in faith with a grateful heart. The Lord is always attentively listening!

Dear Lord,

I want to thank You for Your love for me! Even when I cannot see, You are working to help me. You know the best plans for me. My faith is growing with each prayer I pray. I am trusting You with all my heart, even when I do not understand. I will continue to faithfully pray. I know You see things I cannot see and You know how everything will work out. I am praying about everything with a grateful heart! "*May he grant you your heart's desire and fulfill all your plans*!" Psalm 20:4

In Jesus' Name, Amen

June 18

Are You Facing Everything with God?

The Lord wants us to face everything and rise with Him to a place of faith. He does not want us to fear. When we let fear set in, we forget His promises and run away from God. He wants us to come closer and pray to Him. He has much to show us! The Lord our God is with us wherever we go. Be strong and courageous and you will be victorious! God is with you. He is ready to strengthen you and uphold you with His righteous right hand. Take His hand and let His peace flood your heart. Let your faith rise over fear and you will see the victory!

Dear Lord,

You have given me courage as I let my faith rise over fear. I am letting go of fear so that I can hold on to Your peace. The victory over fear is clear when I trust You. I am ready to go in faith as I walk hand in hand with You one step at a time. When I am afraid, I put my trust in You! *"When I am afraid, I put my trust in you."* Psalm 56:3.

In Jesus' Name, Amen

June 19

Do You See?

Do you see the miracles around you? God has made you to see with spiritual eyes. Are your eyes open to see? God handcrafted you to experience the beauty of the earth and all its creations. Open the eyes of your heart so you can see His wonder and glory! There are miracles all around us as we open our eyes to see and believe the one who has measured the waters in the hollows of His hand and marked off the heavens with a span!

Dear Lord,

I believe You have made me with eyes to see Your glory! I am thankful for You and Your love for me! I know You will answer my prayers as I pray for You to open the eyes of my heart, Lord. All that Your hand touches comes to life with Your light of hope. The darkness disappears when Your light shines brightly for all to see. I am in awe of Your powerful love and peace that calm my heart and rejuvenate my soul! *"Who has measured the waters in the hollow of his hand and marked off the heavens with a span?"* Isaiah 40:12

In Jesus' Name, Amen

June 20

Do You Want to be Revived?

Is your heart heavy with burdens? Seek the Lord and He will touch your heart. Are you stressed and cannot seem to find peace? When you seek the Lord, He will put a new spirit within you to calm your soul. Are you struggling with doubt? Open your heart and let your faith arise! You are not alone when you have the Lord in Your life! He loves us with an everlasting and unconditional love. Rise to new life with the Lord who loves you!

Dear Lord,

You have put Your Spirit within me and given me new life as I have made You my Lord. Thank You for changing my heart and putting a new Spirit within me the very day I trusted You to be my Savior! As I make You my priority, I grow closer to you. I am Your child of light with a new heart and spirit! *"And I will give you a new heart, and a new spirit I will put within you. And I will remove the heart of stone from your flesh and give you a heart of flesh,"* Ezekiel 36:26.

In Jesus' Name, Amen

June 21

Are You Unsure of the Path to Take?

Where is your heart? Have you given the Lord your heart? He is waiting to fill you with spiritual blessings as you make Him Lord of your life. He is ready to journey with you in your life. He will never lead you down the wrong path. Trust Him and give Him your whole heart. Life's demands and challenges can be difficult, but with the Lord, you will rise above it all and know the right way to go!

Dear Lord,

I have plans in my heart. You know them well as You know my heart like no one else. You want the best for me and will show me the way as I follow You. Help me to surrender to You, my Lord and Savior. I have areas in my life I have not given over to you. Help me as I let go and let you show me the way! Your joy has filled my heart as I say yes to Your perfect timing and plan for me! *"The heart of a man plans his way, but the LORD establishes his steps,"* Proverbs 16:9.

In Jesus' Name, Amen

June 22

Are You Facing Temptation?

Are you being watchful to not let sin take hold of you? Where do you turn when you are tempted? The Lord wants to help you say no to harmful decisions. He wants to turn your temptations into opportunities to grow closer to His love and grace. He has forgiven your past and wants you to press on with Him in your present and your future. There is a future of hope waiting for you in the arms of Jesus Christ! Say *yes* to His love and power. He will fight your battles of the flesh!

Dear Lord,

My flesh is weak, but You are my strength. I know I can come to You anytime I face temptation and You will help me find a way out. I do not have to fear when I have You near and the right choice is clear. Everything will be alright when I have Your Spirit working in my life! "*Watch and pray that you may not enter into temptation. The spirit indeed is willing, but the flesh is weak,*" Matthew 26:41.

In Jesus' Name, Amen

June 23

Have You Tried Praying Instead of Fighting?

Are you tired of fighting? Let the Lord fight for you! Have you used your secret weapon of prayer? Ask the Lord for what you need and believe He will answer you! Stop worrying and keep praying for what is on your heart. The Lord already knows exactly what you need even before you ask. When you are armed with prayer and the Word of God, you will be ready for anything you will face. Stand firm, pray, and see the victory!

Dear Lord,

I am in awe as I trust You to fight for me. I believe the battles I face are not mine, but Yours to fight. You want me to be still and know You are God. I believe You will work things out for my good and Your glory. I will trust You one step at a time, one day at a time. I will go when You say go and stay when You say stay. I am still before You as I wait in peace for Your guidance. *"The LORD will fight for you, and you have only to be silent,"* Exodus 14:14.

In Jesus' Name, Amen

June 24

Is the Lord Your Compass?

Do you need grace right now? God is the giver of grace. Trust Him to help you right when you need it. God has fully forgiven you and wants to be your compass. Examine your heart and trust the Lord so He can show you the way. Jesus will be your compass when you let Him guide you out of the wilderness. You are never lost or out of range in His abundant love and constant grace! Do you see the way now as you pray?

Dear Lord,

I am bowing before You with a humble heart of thanksgiving. I know You have fully forgiven me, and my soul is at peace. I can rest in Your love knowing there is nothing I can do to make You love me less. Your grace has saved me. I am trusting You, Lord, the lifter of my soul and keeper of my heart. Your everlasting love and amazing grace give me greater hope. Your promises are written on my heart and my soul. I *do* trust You and I *do* believe! *"To you, O LORD, I lift up my soul, O my God, in you I trust..."* Psalm 25:1-2.

In Jesus' Name, Amen

June 25

Are You Listening?

Have you ever wondered why the Lord seemed silent in your life? Have you cried out to the Lord with passion for what is on your heart? Have you been actively listening? When you ask Him for what is on your heart, the Lord is listening to you. He will speak if you open your heart to listen. He will put the answers before you in His Word. He wants you to come closer to His love and grace. Begin today by opening your Bible and your heart as you are still before the Lord. Be still and know that He is God so He will speak to your heart!

Dear Lord,

I know You hear my prayers and will speak to me as I listen. I am so thankful for Your amazing love that instills peace in my soul. I hear You calling me to step out in faith as I trust You. I step out with open ears, eyes, and heart, Lord. I will keep my mind clear of negativity so I can hear You speaking truth. *"Pay attention to what you hear: with the measure you use, it will be measured to you..."* Mark 4:24.

In Jesus' Name, Amen

June 26

Do You Believe the Promises of God?

The Lord gives us promises and will do what He says He will do. For us to hear, we must wake up and listen. The Lord wants us to rise and do what He has instructed us to do. There are times when we are tempted to question or doubt before we act because we do not see or understand. But when we are faithful and still before our Lord, He will show us great and mighty things as He speaks truth to us. In the truth, there is peace, hope, and joy! Be still before the Lord and obey his instructions to you.

Dear Lord,

As I am still before You, I can hear You. I have been listening to Your promises and believing each one. It is good to see with eyes fixed upon You. I see things You have been wanting to show me. I am still before You, Lord, eager to listen. I believe You can do what seems impossible! I know You will do what You say You will do, my Lord and Savior. *"Be still, and know that I am God,"* Psalm 46:10.

In Jesus' Name, Amen

June 27

Did You Know You Are Rich?

The Lord knows your heart. He knows your thoughts and knows what you need even before you ask. Even when you make mistakes, He will forgive you and give you the richness of His grace and mercy. Have you sinned and fallen short of the glory of God? Even so, God still loves You and has given you grace: *God's Riches At Christ's Expense.* What a glorious gift of riches He has given us! You are rich in Christ!

Dear Lord,

Thank You for giving me a heart to know and love You. Examine my heart to see if there is anything that is not pleasing to You. Help me to run away from those things and turn closer to You. I know there is great gain when I am living in Your love with the mind of Christ. I am content when You are the center of my life! My mind is set on You! *"Search me, O God, and know my heart! Try me and know my thoughts!"* Psalm 139:23.

In Jesus' Name, Amen

June 28

Do You Believe God Will Move Mountains?

God has the power to do more than we could ever imagine. He wants us to trust Him and be obedient one step at a time. When we are, He directs our path. The blessings from God are abundant and amazing! He wants us to trust Him so He can show us more of his plans for us. Watch Him move in your life as you trust and obey. He will show you His glory as His blessings abound all around you. God will amaze you! Get ready for the Lord to empower you and move mountains!

Dear Lord,

I believe You can do anything! Obedience will bring me closer to You and Your will. My faith is stronger, and my joy is indescribable when I have Your power active inside me. You speak to the mountains and they move! How powerful and great you are, Lord! *"Now to him who is able to do far more abundantly than all we can ask or think, according to the power at work within us,"* Ephesians 3:20.

In Jesus' Name, Amen

June 29

Do You Believe God's Glory Shines Brightest in the Darkness?

Have you lost your hope because of what you see around you? Have you given up because of the uncertainty in the world? There is hope even in these uncertain times. God has promised you He will never leave or forsake you. Even when others abandon you, God will remain faithful and true to *you*! He loves you, dear one. His glory shines brightest in the darkness. When it seems there is no hope, He is there! Believe His promises, be still, and know He is God!

Dear Lord,

I believe You will never leave or forsake me. I am the only one who can separate myself from Your love. You ask that I trust You, so You can make me free and alive with Your hand upon me. I will stay focused on the hope I have in You. I am thankful for Your never-ending promises that encourage my heart and enrich my soul. I will wait for You, Lord! *"I wait for the LORD, my soul waits, and in his word I hope,"* Psalm 130:5.

In Jesus' Name, Amen

June 30

Is God Your Refuge?

Are you trusting the Lord? Have you reached out to Him in prayer? He sees your struggles and knows your heart. In the stillness of your soul, He is there. As you come even closer, His presence fills the depths of your soul. As you let Him lead you, He will show you the path to take. Why are you trying to do everything by yourself? Trust the Lord with all your heart and He will guide you in the direction that leads to life in Him.

Dear Lord,

I know you will help me as I trust and obey you. You want the best for me. As I put You in the center of my life, I see your glory and I feel your presence lighting my way. I am grateful for the answers you have given me. I am humbled by your grace and encouraged by your love. I have confidence You will answer my prayers. As I faithfully pray, I will trust you more and more each day! *"Trust in him at all times, O people; pour out your heart before him; God is a refuge for us,"* Psalm 62:8.

In Jesus' Name, Amen

Monthly Reflections

As you pray and lean on the Lord's promises, write what the Lord has revealed to you for this month.

REJOICE IN HOPE,
be patient
in tribulation,
be constant
IN PRAYER.
ROMANS 12:12

July 1

Are You Seeking the Presence of the Lord?

When we seek the presence of the Lord, we will find refreshment. He renews us when we cling to Jesus Christ. He waits for us to come to Him so He can renew our hearts and refresh our souls. Our Lord wants us to come to Him. He yearns for us to be close to Him. As we run to the Father for a renewed relationship, He will open His arms and welcome us. He is waiting for you!

Dear Lord,

Oh, how I love You, Lord! Your love has changed me to be the person You want me to be. As I open my heart, You refresh my soul. I am walking closer to You, my Lord and Savior. I am secure with every step I take because of my faith in You. I will walk with You as I navigate these waters. I am not afraid when I hold Your hand. I am refreshed and revived by Your presence! *"Times of refreshing may come from the presence of the Lord, and that He may send the Christ appointed for you, Jesus,"* Acts 3:20.

In Jesus' Name, Amen

July 2

Is Your Heart Full of Joy?

Give thanks to the Lord for His joy! As you walk in His truth, you will find His steadfast love brings *so* much joy. As you draw to His presence, you will find there is fullness of joy in your soul. Discover the abundant life of joy in Christ that awaits you. He is waiting for you. Let go and find the joy that is yours in Jesus. There is joy in the journey when you journey with Jesus!

Dear Lord,

I feel Your joy deep inside me as I seek You, Lord. Your joy fills me and all is well with my soul. As I cling tighter to You, I can rest. As I am still, You speak truth and life to me. As I breathe in Your love, You awaken me to new life and greater joy! I know this joy only comes from Your hands upon me! You have restored my soul! *"For you, O LORD, have made me glad by your work; at the works of your hands I sing for joy,"* Psalm 92:4.

In Jesus' Name, Amen

July 3

Are You Dwelling in the Shelter of God?

God wants you to rest. He sees you struggling. He sees you are restless. He offers His peace to you. When you lie down to sleep, He is with you. When you are wide awake, He is with you. The Lord is watching over you. Find your rest in His loving arms! God will comfort your soul and help you sleep. When you are restless, God will give you peace. When you are hopeless, God will give you courage. When you are struggling, God will give you strength.

Dear Lord,

I will find my security and rest as I press into You. I lift my prayers to You and ask You to strengthen me. I am certain You will help me sleep when I take my focus off of my problems and start pressing into Your peace. I have been holding on to things I cannot change instead of handing them over to You and trusting You. You are my dwelling place, Lord. You bring me rest. *"In peace I will both lie down and sleep; for you alone, O LORD, make me dwell in safety,"* Psalm 4:8.

In Jesus' Name, Amen

July 4

Are You Seeking Wisdom from the Lord?

Are you seeking the Lord to guide you? Have you yearned for a heart of wisdom? Let the Lord guide you into all truth. His wisdom comes to those who trust and obey Him. As you turn your heart toward Christ and center your life on Him, you will find a peace that will settle in your soul. The eyes of your heart will see God and you will have clearer direction. Listen to the Holy Spirit speak through His Word. Are you actively listening?

Dear Lord,

When I am looking for wisdom, I will look to You. I hear Your voice in my spirit telling me what to do. Even when I do not understand, I will trust you and obey Your promptings. You will give me wisdom that brings peace to my soul. My days are full of life as I eagerly seek Your way. Wisdom will come as I press into You, let go of the distractions around me, and let You speak to me. *"So teach us to number our days, that we may get a heart of wisdom,"* Psalm 90:12.

In Jesus' Name, Amen

July 5

Have You Praised the Lord Today?

Are you praising the Lord for all He has done for you? He wants to give you a future and a hope. When you fear the Lord, you are showing Him you love Him. When you trust and obey Him, He can do so many things through you. When you delight in the Lord, and walk by faith, He will transform your life! Want to be all that God has made you to be? Fear the Lord and obey His commandments, starting with the first one; love the Lord your God with all your heart, soul, and mind!

Dear Lord,

I am praising You for all Your goodness and glory! Thank You for all my spiritual blessings from above! As I delight in You, the desires of my heart have changed to be more about You and less about me. I have peace as I walk with You and do what You want me to do. As I walk by faith, joy fills me with more of You! *"Praise the Lord! Blessed is the man who fears the Lord, who greatly delights in his commandments*!" Psalm 112:1.

In Jesus' Name, Amen

July 6

Do You Know You Are Beautiful?

Do you see the beauty around you? Have you noticed the small things that bring joy to your heart? God has created so much for you to enjoy on the earth. He has even more beauty, that we cannot imagine or comprehend, that will be revealed to you in Heaven. Seek first the Kingdom of God, and all these things will be added to you. Look around and see His hand that works miracles. You are one of His beautiful miracles with spiritual blessings and eternal life promised to you if you receive Christ as your Savior!

Dear Lord,

I am praising You for making all things beautiful! I know there is more in store for me if I keep faithfully trusting You. You are so wonderful to me and I am praising You for Your countless blessings! Endless love and amazing grace are lavished upon me! My eyes do see! *"He has made everything beautiful in its time..."* Ecclesiastes 3:11.

In Jesus' Name, Amen

July 7

Are You Living with Regret or Rejoicing with Gratitude?

Are you continuing to worry about things you cannot change? Is life full of regret or filled with gratitude? The Lord has already forgiven you when you have believed. He has wiped away your crimson stains and washed them white as snow. There is nothing you can do to make Him love you less. In Christ, you are forgiven and free. Step out of the darkness of your troubles and defeat and live in the sparkling light with Jesus Christ as your personal Savior!

Dear Lord,

Thank You for taking all my troubles so I can live freely! You have given me life. I trust You. I am thankful for all You have done for me. Instead of living with regret, I choose to live with hope. My faith is growing stronger each day. Your love has conquered my fears and taken away my tears. I am resting in Your presence and it is well with my soul! *"Let not your hearts be troubled. Believe in God; believe also in me,"* John 14:1.

In Jesus' Name, Amen

July 8

Are You Doing the Work God Created for You to Do?

God created us with His workmanship for good works so that we may walk in them. Turn to God and make the most of the opportunities He has given you! Are you trusting the Lord and walking with Him with confidence and security? God wants to show you the path to life. Let Him lead you to victory that is yours in Christ Jesus. All your spiritual blessings are yours in Christ when you say yes and stand on His promises!

Dear Lord,

Thank You for creating me with spiritual blessings. I know You want me to walk in the good works created just for me. As I work, You are fighting my battles and blessing me with power and strength for the challenge. I am walking by faith in the good works which You have given me! *"For we are his workmanship, created in Christ Jesus for good works, which God prepared beforehand, that we should walk in them,"* Ephesians 2:10.

In Jesus' Name, Amen

July 9

Are You Letting Your Light Shine?

The light from the Lord shines in those who have made Him the Lord of their lives. When we believe, His light shines in us. We are children of His light. As we come closer to His love, by trusting and obeying Him, His light shines brightly. Are you sharing your light? Let it shine so all the world can see! The light from Christ brings hope to a broken and lost world. Let it shine brightly as you work for the Lord.

Dear Lord,

You have brightened all my days since I have opened my heart fully to You. I am blessed to have Your unending love. As I shine Your light, I feel alive in a new way as my heart is full of joy! The darkness disappears as Your light touches me. I will keep shining Your light so that others may see You in me. I will let it shine for Your glory! *"Let your light shine before others, so that they may see your good works and give glory to your Father who is in heaven,"* Matthew 5:16.

In Jesus' Name, Amen

July 10

Are You Letting God Calm Your Anxious Heart?

When we are anxious, panic and worry set in. When we let our emotions control us, we worry what might happen. God wants to calm our hearts and bring peace to our souls. Our anxiety will bring fear if we let our emotions control us. Instead of being controlled by the what-ifs of life, let us give our worries to God who will bring us His perfect peace! God can calm your anxious heart one hundred percent of the time if you give Him one hundred percent of you!

Dear Lord,

Thank You for calming my worries and taking my burdens. I give them all to You so You can work them out. You have a plan for my life that does not include my worry. I trust you, Lord. I believe what You have promised me, and I am full of hope and joy! I will not let fear come in but will hold onto faith as You show me the way to freedom and peace! *"And which of you by being anxious can add a single hour to his span of life?"* Matthew 6:27.

In Jesus' Name, Amen

July 11

Do You Have Joy in Your Heart?

Jesus gives us everything we need and more. He is there for us at all times. When we need a friend, He is there. When we need guidance, He is there. When we need encouragement, He is there. When we are lost, He is there. When we have pain, He is there. When we need peace, He is there. When we need joy, He is there. His presence is with us at all times when we seek Him. Are you seeking more of Jesus?

Dear Lord,

Thank You for putting more joy in my heart! I know when I seek Your presence, there will be fullness of joy. At Your right hand, there are pleasures forevermore! I am blessed by You as you fill me with abundant joy deep in my heart! I have joy, joy, joy, joy down in my heart to stay! *"You have put more joy in my heart…"* Psalm 4:7.

In Jesus' Name, Amen

July 12

Do You Want to be Healed?

God wants to heal us. He *can* heal us. When we need healing, we can trust the one who has promised healing. He is waiting for us to reach out with hands of faith and ask in prayer. Only God knows how we need to be healed. Do you need the touch of God upon you? Are you ready for the healing God has for you? Stretch out your hand of faith and let God touch you. Lift your heart to the Healer who has healing in His hands for you!

Dear Lord,

I believe You can heal me. I know my healing is in Your hands. I am sure of what I hope for, and certain of what I cannot see. You are listening to my prayers and I know the healing has begun. I will continue to earnestly pray for what is on my heart. I will not stop praying, and believing, for healing that is mine in You! As I lift my heart and my hands to You, I am revived and restored! *"Stretch out your hand..."* Mark 3:5.

In Jesus' Name, Amen

July 13

Are You on the Path that Leads to Life?

The road less traveled is narrow. Not many will enter it. But those who do, will find life! The Lord will lead those who choose to walk with Him. They will find Him present on this path. Come walk on the road with the Lord. In the presence of the Lord there is fullness of joy! He will continue to bless those who make Him Lord of their lives. Are you on the path that leads to life?

Dear Lord,

I know the path to life is narrow but that those who walk on it will find life. I have found when I journey with You, Lord, my life is filled with great joy. I know that You can do more than I could ever dream or imagine as I fully trust You. In the waiting, my faith has come alive. I have been transformed by Your redeeming love. Your presence brings me peace and patience that the world cannot give. It is well with my soul! *"For the gate is narrow and the way is hard that leads to life, and those who find it are few,"* Matthew 7:14.

In Jesus' Name, Amen

July 14

Is Your Soul Waiting for the Lord?

God wants us to wait upon Him. In the waiting, God has much to show us. He wants us to abide in Him so He can show us His plans for us. While we wait on Him, we will find new strength, His purpose for us, His perfect plan for our life, and living hope. All of this is possible when we put our full faith and trust in God. Be still and wait upon God to find your way!

Dear Lord,

While I wait, I will worship You! I know You are transforming me to be who you want me to be. As I trust You more, You will reveal Your plan and purpose for me. I will seek Your presence instead of questioning Your perfect timing. I will find lasting hope and greater faith as I wait upon Your promises. "*I wait for the Lord, my soul waits, and in his word I hope,*" Psalm 130:5.

In Jesus' Name, Amen

July 15

Is God Doing Something New in You?

Do you see that the former things have come to pass? God is creating something new in you. There is new hope for what God is going to do in you. He is waiting for you to lean on Him and let the Holy Spirit come to life in you. Come closer and let His love touch your heart and soul. Trust the Lord with all your heart and see His plan for you come to life!

Dear Lord,

I want to come closer to You. I know that Your love will enrich my life when I trust and obey You. I am holding on to Your hope by holding on to You. There is greater hope when I lean on You. Thank You for doing something new in me. I trust You completely. The old has passed away and the new has come! *"Behold, the former things have come to pass, and new things I now declare; before they spring forth I tell you of them,"* Isaiah 42:9.

In Jesus' Name, Amen

July 16

Do You Know a Relationship with the Lord Will Renew You?

There is pain in this world. There are struggles and challenges. Even when we do not understand, God is healing. He is working all things out for His glory so His people will be healed. He wants a renewed relationship with His children. He yearns for all to come closer to His love. Do you want to be healed? God wants to heal your body *and* your soul. He has been waiting for you to come to Him. As you ask the Lord, He will attend to the voice of your prayers. There is complete healing for you in the arms of your Lord and Savior, Jesus Christ

Dear Lord,

I know You are healing me as I turn my face towards You. I am stronger now than I have ever been because I am focusing on You and living in Your love. It is well with my soul as I soak up the healing! *"Beloved, I pray that all may go well with you and that you may be in good health, as it goes well with your soul,"* 3 John 2.

In Jesus' Name, Amen

July 17

Do You Know the Love of Christ that Heals?

Love makes the heart grow. A heart of love pleases our Lord. When we love others, we show our love for Him. He knows our hearts and wants us to love others like He loves us. He has forgiven us with the sacrifice of His love that covers a multitude of sins. When we seek the Lord and receive His love and forgiveness, we will find His love touching all the places of our heart. Then we can freely love and forgive others. Are you having trouble forgiving others because you are not forgiving yourself? Trust Jesus and know He loves you and has forgiven you!

Dear Lord,

Thank You for loving me. You have put Your seal upon my heart, and I am rejoicing in hope! It is so good to be loved by You, Lord! I know I am forgiven, and I am free! I will love others as You have loved me. There is a future of love as I trust in You and Your promises! *"Above all, keep loving one another earnestly, since love covers a multitude of sins,"* 1 Peter 4:8.

In Jesus' Name, Amen

July 18

Do You Believe Nothing is Impossible with God?

God can do anything! Nothing is too hard for Him! When we put our complete trust in Him, He will show us great and mighty things He wants to do *in* and *through* us! Have you been waiting for an answer from God? Are you believing He can do the impossible for you? Keep praying for what you hope for but do not yet see. Let your faith rise above your doubt. God will do what He says He will do. There is nothing too hard for Him! As you lean on God, He will help you rise!

Dear Lord,

I know You will make a way when it seems there isn't one. You have conquered death, and nothing is impossible for You, Lord. I am not afraid of the future but will step up and step out to meet You where there is hope for me. I believe You will do the impossible! *"Ah, Lord GOD! It is you who has made the heavens and the earth by your great power and by your outstretched arm! Nothing is too hard for you,"* Jeremiah 32:17.

In Jesus' Name, Amen

July 19

Who is Your Rock?

Are you weary from all the problems around you? Have you lost your faith because of fear? Turn to the Lord, your rock and refuge. He will be there for you no matter what you are facing. He knows what is happening to you. The challenges you are facing are avenues for you to come closer to your rock of salvation. He will strengthen you for any trial in your life. Only God can bring you through it all. Lean on Him and find refuge in God. Trust Him and let your faith grow!

Dear Lord,

There are days when I struggle to keep going. My faith in You, Lord, my fortress and my refuge, is the only way I can make it through the day. You are higher than any problem I will ever face and You are a present help in trouble. You have delivered me and have given me hope even on the most difficult days. *"The LORD is my rock and my fortress and my deliverer, my God, my rock, in whom I take refuge, my shield, and the horn of my salvation, my stronghold,,"* Psalm 18:2.

In Jesus' Name, Amen

July 20

Are You Setting Your Mind on the Spirit?

When we set our mind on the Spirit, we will find life and peace. God wants us to keep drawing towards Him by setting our hearts on Him. When we let the Holy Spirit lead us, we will discover a life full of hope that is ours in Christ. You have a choice as to which way you will live. God has given us His Spirit so we can live in Him! Turn away from the flesh that leads to sin and turn back to the hope that is yours in Christ! Come closer to His love and set your mind and your heart on the Spirit of God!

Dear Lord,

I am full of peace and hope as I draw to You and live in tune with the Holy Spirit, Lord. Thank You for showing me the way as I keep my mind on You. I will fix my heart and mind on You more each day to live in the power and presence of the Holy Spirit! *"To set the mind on the flesh is death, but to set the mind on the Spirit is life and peace,"* Romans 8:6.

In Jesus' Name, Amen

July 21

Do You Know the Eye
of the Lord is Upon You?

The Lord sees us and wants to guide us. He has His eye upon all of us and sees everything we do. He will help direct us on the way we should go. We just need to follow Him. It is so good to be led by God who wants the best for us. Take hold of His hand. He will never abandon or forget us. He is always faithful to us. Will you be faithful to Him? The best is yet to come!

Dear Lord,

Thank You for showing me the way. I see the path You want me to take and I will walk in it. There is no fear when I put faith first. You are helping me with each step I take. I will stay faithful. I will listen and I will walk in Your way. I will let You take hold of my hand and lead me to my destiny! "*I will instruct you and teach you in the way you should go; I will counsel you with my eye upon you*," Psalm 32:8.

In Jesus' Name, Amen

July 22

What is Your Calling?

Are you wondering why you are living where you are? Do you believe God has a purpose and a plan for your life? God has put you here for such a time as this. He wants you to walk by faith in His purpose and His plan for you. Your next step is just a prayer away. Once you start seeking God's plan for your life, He will give you clear direction! It is time to step into your destiny!

Dear Lord,

I am thankful for Your purpose and plan for me! I know You have placed me right where I am for such a time as this. I will keep praying for more instructions as I walk by faith each step of the way. You always make a way despite obstacles that may block my path. You make my path straight. I trust You more each day! *"And who knows whether you have not come to the kingdom for such a time as this?"* Esther 4:14.

In Jesus' Name, Amen

July 23

Are You Serving God with a Surrendered Heart?

God wants you to surrender all and serve Him. He wants you to show your love for Him by obeying His commandments and walking in His ways. Surrender and serve the Lord who loves you and gives grace. His perfect peace will touch your heart as you let go and let Him love you. If you keep running away, you will never know the peace that is possible through a relationship with God. Surrender, open your heart, and let His love touch your heart!

Dear Lord,

You want us all to live in love. Peace is possible as I let go of offense, hate, and bitterness and let Your love in every place of my heart. I am praying for the peace of God to enter the hearts of all. It is time to let go and surrender all to You, Lord. Even when my eyes cannot see, I have faith in what only You can do. There is nothing impossible for You! *"But as for me and my house, we will serve the Lord,"* Joshua 24:15.

In Jesus' Name, Amen

July 24

Are You Praying and Praising the Lord with Others?

       Are you continuing to pray? Jesus hears your prayers and is glorified when you pray in His name in unity with other believers. Is your heart and soul open to pray with others? Where two or more are gathered in the name of Jesus, He is there. He wants us to pray together and *believe* together. His power and presence are real in our lives as we pray! Communicate with the Lord, your God, through Jesus Christ, and lift your prayers to Him! He is there for you and will attend to your needs!

Dear Lord,

       It is refreshing to pray and feel Your calming peace. Even when there is chaos around me, Your present peace floods my soul. I will continue to pray with others as well. There is power as we pray in the name of Jesus. Lord, help us live in peace and unity with hearts to love each other! Thank You for attending to the voice of my prayers! *"For where two or three are gathered in my name, there I am among them,"* Matthew 18:20.

In Jesus' Name, Amen

July 25

Do You Know the Spirit of the Lord Dwells Inside You?

Are you tired of the unrest around you? Have you been stressed about what you cannot control? Activate the Spirit who dwells inside you. Trust His guidance and step out in faith. The world and its ways cannot overcome you. You are more than a conqueror with the presence and power of the Holy Spirit living inside you. Your body is a temple where the Holy Spirit dwells. Let go and let God touch your heart. Listen with your heart and He will give you hope once again!

Dear Lord,

I know there are things around me that are out of control. Instead of focusing on what I cannot change, I will pray for Your hand to touch hearts and souls. Only You can help us, Lord! I will cling to You, my Lord and Savior! In You there is fullness of joy and the presence of peace! *"Or do you not know that your body is a temple of the Holy Spirit within you, whom you have from God?"* 1 Corinthians 6:19.

In Jesus' Name, Amen

July 26

Where is Your Faith?

God wants us to have faith and not be afraid. He yearns for us to trust Him so He can grow our faith. As we come closer to Him with our whole hearts, our fears will subside, and our faith will increase. God wants to show us the way to victory through faith. All we need to do is make the choice to trust Him wholeheartedly. Put your faith and trust in the living God who is the only way to a life without fear! Why are you so afraid?

Dear Lord,

I am sure of what I hope for even when I do not see only because of my faith in You! You, Lord, are the only way to live a life of great faith. When I keep trusting You, my heart comes closer to Your love. I know You are ready to show me more as I trust You. Even when it does not make sense to me, I will keep my faith in You. Your way is the only way! *"Why are you so afraid? Have you still no faith?"* Mark 4:40.

In Jesus' Name, Amen

July 27

Do You Know God's Love?

Love is the greatest gift. God loves us so much that He gave us Jesus, His only Son. We are *loved*. It is amazing to be loved by God who knows every one of us and loves us with an everlasting love! Do you know the love of the Father? Have you given Him your whole heart? He wants you to know Him and believe that He loves you! Only God can help you overcome. His love is the key that opens the heart. He who is in you is greater than He who is in the world! You are more than a conqueror with the love of Jesus inside you!

Dear Lord,

Thank You for loving me. I know the greatest gift of Your love, Jesus. I am stronger when You are with me. Your love has given me hope as I step out in faith. I know the truth of Your eternal love and it has set me free! Your love remains forever in me as I abide in You! *"So now faith, hope, and love abide, these three; but the greatest of these is love,"* 1 Corinthians 13:13.

In Jesus' Name, Amen

July 28

Are You Confused and Worried?

Are you confused and worried about what you see? Have you lost your hope because you are afraid? God has given you a Spirit of love and not fear. He wants you to climb that mountain by faith and with God's strength. He will not fail you even when all the odds are against you. God is fighting your battles; you must just be silent and let Him fight for you. The victory is yours in Christ!

Dear Lord,

I am ready to listen and let You fight for me. I have partially let go but want to fully surrender to You. Only You can conquer my giants. You are greater than anything I will face. I am going to let go and keep praying without ceasing! There are more prayers left for me to pray and more answers to come! It is in the stillness of my soul that I see You! Thank You for rescuing me! I love You, Lord, my Prince of Peace! *"For God is not a God of confusion but of peace,"* 1 Corinthians 14:33.

In Jesus' Name, Amen

July 29

Do You Know You Are Blessed
by the Grace of God?

God has blessed us by His amazing grace. We have salvation through our Lord Jesus Christ who died and rose from the grave so that we can live in freedom! Our blessings are found in the arms of our Savior. Why do we cling to other things and not the hope of glory? Why is it hard to let go and let God have His way in us? The struggle with sin is real, but we can overcome when we cling to the real hope of Jesus Christ!

Dear Lord,

I know You have called me to let go of my selfish desires and let You work in me. I will surrender all to You, Lord, so that You can make old things new! It is a new day for me to be lavished by Your grace. It is by grace that I have been saved. I am who I am because of Your grace! I am blessed by Your saving grace! *"But by the grace of God I am what I am, and his grace toward me was not in vain,"* 1 Corinthians 15:10.

In Jesus' Name, Amen

July 30

Do You Know Jesus
will be with You Forever?

Are life's issues bringing you down? Is trouble knocking at your door? Instead of opening the door to negativity, open the door to life and positivity by letting Jesus reign inside you. He has been trying to get your attention all your life. Did you see Him today when your child said, "I love you!" or when your neighbor offered to help you get through a hard time? Did you notice the joy you felt when your dog greeted you as you came in the door or when your cat purred in your lap? These gifts are from Jesus. He wants you to love Him so that He can fill you with utmost joy!

Dear Lord,

These days are challenging but I am thankful I have You in my life! You have comforted me and helped me get through difficult days. I am free falling into Your arms of love as I love You with all my heart and soul! I know that you will be with me forever! *"And behold, I am with you always, to the end of the age,"* Matthew 28:20.

In Jesus' Name, Amen

July 31

Do You Need Protection?

When you need protection, the Lord will be a present help. He commands His angels to cover you and protect you from harm. He will give you peace right when you need it most. As trouble comes near, God comes closer. God sees what you are going through and wants to help you. The Lord wants to rescue you, so take His hand and walk with Him to a place of rest and security. There is a hiding place for you in the presence of God! The Spirit of God is present in those who believe! Trust God and find refuge in Him!

Dear Lord,

Your hand has saved me. It is in Your presence I find my refuge and peace. I know You will strengthen me for what lies ahead. You have given me a glimpse of heaven when I see wonders of Your love around me. Thank You for sending Your angels to protect me. I will cling to You and Your promises! *"For he will command his angels concerning you to guard you in all your ways,"* Psalm 91:11.

In Jesus' Name, Amen

Monthly Reflections

As you pray and lean on the Lord's promises, write
what the Lord has revealed to you for this month.

For nothing
WILL BE
IMPOSSIBLE
with God.
LUKE 1:37

August 1

Do You Want to be Set Free?

Are you ready to be set free? Have you trusted the Lord with all your heart? Trust the Lord and *believe* to receive your freedom! You have been given grace upon grace so you can know His love. Give grace to others and grace will be given to you. Forgive and you will be forgiven. Love and you will be loved. If you choose the way of Jesus, you will be set free. When the Son sets you free, you will be free, indeed!

Dear Lord,

I know Your freedom as I have believed in You. Your grace has brought light to the darkness and saved me from sin. I am worthy because You say I am. I am loved because You first loved me. I am set free because You died for me. I am secure because You rose from the grave for me. I am born again into new life because of Your grace and love for me! *"So if the Son sets you free, you will be free indeed,"* John 8:36.

In Jesus' Name, Amen

August 2

Do You Need Comfort and Peace?

Are you looking for restoration and peace? Do you need the comfort of the Lord? Pray for His peace to reign in you and let Him comfort you. He loves you and wants to see you smile again. It's been too long since you have felt joy. Step back into His presence and make the Lord the first love of your life! He will wipe away your tears and put joy back into your heart! There is joy and peace to discover in the presence of God as you aim for restoration!

Dear Lord,

You want me to find comfort and peace in You. It is in Your presence that I will find my strength to press on. Your peace will come to me as I wait upon You and find my refuge in You. My soul will find rest as I let go and let You lead me where You want me to go. I am revived and restored by You, Lord! Hallelujah! *"Finally brothers, rejoice. Aim for restoration, comfort one another, agree with one another, live in peace, and the God of love and peace will be with you,"* 2 Corinthians 13:11.

In Jesus' Name, Amen

August 3

Have You Praised the Lord
for His Love and Grace?

The Lord has blessed us richly with His love and grace. He has shown us His glory in so many ways. He wants to hear our praise and thankfulness as we lift our voices up to Him with grateful hearts. The beauty of His love is magnified all around us. Pursue Him and you will find Him! Take a look around you and be filled with the hope and beauty of the Lord that shines brilliantly!

Dear Lord,

I believe You will show me Your glory as I grow in faith and love. I will praise You, even when my eyes cannot see, because I know You are working around me. As I walk by faith, You will show me greater glory. All things are possible with You! I am sure of what I hope for and certain of what I do not yet see! I believe! Hallelujah! *"From the rising of the sun to its setting, the name of the LORD is to be praised!"* Psalm 113:3.

In Jesus' Name, Amen

August 4

Do You Need to Take Time to Rest?

When you are weary and burdened, you will live in a state of distress and anxiety. You have done your best to keep going in this state of chaos because this world tells you to keep running no matter what. But the Lord Jesus tells you to slow down and find your rest in Him. He will give you the rest you need when you call upon Him. Only Jesus can shield you from distress. Come to Him in your weariness and find all you need in Him! Take heart when the troubles of the world are weighing you down, because the Lord will take your burdens and be your rock of refuge and strength!

Dear Lord,

I am weary and tired of trying to carry all my burdens alone. You have promised to take them and give me rest and refuge. I will give You my burdens and take Your yoke of strength and power. Thank You for helping me find all I need in You! I am finally still in Your presence, Lord, and praising You for being my hope and peace! *"Come to me, all who labor and are heavy laden, and I will give you rest,"* Matthew 11:28.

In Jesus' Name, Amen

August 5

Do You Know the Truth?

Do you want to know the truth so you can live in freedom? God has given you His Son, Jesus Christ, so you can be set free. Jesus died and rose from the grave and lives inside of all who make Him the Lord of their lives. There are multiple paths we can venture down, but only one way that will set us free; the cross of Christ is the way to truth. Find your freedom and the fullness of new life the truth of Christ. Come home to Jesus so you can truly be free!

Dear Lord,

Thank You for the truth that has set me free! It is so good to know the power of Your love and Your truth! I will walk in hope as I abide in Your Word and set my mind on the things above that are eternal and true instead of focusing on what I cannot change. The Son has set me free, so I am free, indeed! *"If you abide in my word, you are truly my disciples, and you will know the truth, and the truth will set you free,"* John 8:31-32.

In Jesus' Name, Amen

August 6

Have You Been Faithful
in the Little Things?

Are you hopeful even when you cannot see? Have you stayed faithful in the little things? God sees your heart and your faith. He will bless you as you stay faithful. He will set you over much as you grow in your faith. Keep looking to the Lord because He can do more in and through You when you surrender and let your faith shine. It is time to do all He has called you to do. Listen with your heart and give God your *best yes* by being faithful in the little things.

Dear Lord,

I know You see my faith. You want me to stay faithful in the small things. I will stay focused on You and keep my faith alive. I am hopeful for what I believe and certain of what You can do in and through me. Thank You for helping me see hope through my faith in You! I will keep stepping out in faith one step at a time! "*Well done, good and faithful servant. You have been faithful over little; I will set you over much. Enter into the joy of your master,*" Matthew 25:23.

In Jesus' Name, Amen

August 7

Do You Need to be Rescued?

God wants you to call upon Him. He will restore and rescue you when you need help. Do not be afraid to ask Him for what is on your heart. He is listening and will speak love to you. What has you down? Have you brought it before the Lord your God? Nothing is too hard for your Lord! Try asking and see what happens! *"But I call to God, and the LORD will save me,"* Psalm 55:16.

Dear Lord,

I hear You in the depth of my soul telling me, "Keep praying and then be watchful in it with thanksgiving. Do not give up but get ready for what I am about to do! Be prepared for greater blessings that will come as you trust me in everything!" I do trust You, Lord! Thank You for saving me!

In Jesus' Name, Amen

August 8

Do You Want Mercy, Peace, and Love
to be Multiplied to You?

Are you trusting the Lord with all your heart so He can multiply mercy? Are you looking to the Lord for your peace instead of drowning in the fear of what might happen? Let the love of the Lord hold you up when life brings you down. Jesus inside you is greater than the world around you. Only Jesus can multiply mercy, peace, and love to you eternally. Trust Him to do what is impossible for man!

Dear Lord,

I am so thankful for You and Your love for me. Your mercy reigns true! It is so good to be loved by You as Your peace calms my soul. I am trusting You and believing what You say to me. I know You can do what seems impossible and You will do what You promise. I am trusting You and am so thankful I am Your child who believes! *"May mercy, peace, and love be multiplied to you,"* Jude 2.

In Jesus' Name, Amen

August 9

Are You Praying for All People?

God hears your prayers, and He wants you to lift up your prayers for all people. He hears you as the Holy Spirit intercedes. Use your powerful weapon of prayer. You can carry your faith as you lift up others to God in prayer. Are you faithfully praying for those on your heart? Keep lifting your voice in prayer by praying for what is on your heart. Take your troubles and worries and turn them into prayers. God is listening and loves to hear you pray!

Dear Lord,

I know You hear me when I pray. I have confidence I can face my giants with the weapon of prayer you have given me. I will keep my prayers coming for other people so You can answer my supplications. You attend patiently to the voice of my prayers. You help me conquer all my fears as I pray. Peace enters my soul as I lift my voice to You! *"First of all, then, I urge that supplications, prayers, intercessions, and thanksgivings be made for all people,"* 1 Timothy 2:1.

In Jesus' Name, Amen

August 10

Are You Searching for Answers?

We have a God in heaven who reveals mysteries. He has all the answers and speaks truth to those who listen. When we do not understand, He gives us glimpses of hope. When we struggle, He is there for us. He reveals promises in His timing and in His will. He loves all His children and wants us to come closer to His love. Are you ready to listen? He is speaking to you.

Dear Lord,

Thank You for showing up and showing Your glory to all who are ready to see! I am so thankful for every glimpse of heaven You reveal. In the beautiful sunsets, I see You. In the stars at night, I see You. In the smiles of other people, I see You. In the helping hands that serve, I see You. In the eyes that are filled with compassion, I see You. In the hearts that give love, I see You. *"But there is a God in heaven who reveals mysteries…"* Daniel 2:28.

In Jesus' Name, Amen

August 11

Have You Given Your Heart to the Lord?

Are you ready to come home to the Lord? You have been running away and trying to do life on your own. Do you know that Jesus loves you and wants you to come home to Him? He sees your heart and knows your fears. He will comfort and fully strengthen you. He will heal you from the inside out. Turn around and take the first step back to Jesus! He has loved you through it all and wants to speak love into your life. Are you ready to come home?

Dear Lord,

Thank You for healing me! I have seen You work miracles. I lean into You and pray. You want to do something new in me. I must return to You with all my heart! I am growing in grace and truth as I let go and let You have Your way in me! It is well with my soul as I return to You! *"Return to me with all your heart…"* Joel 2:12.

In Jesus' Name, Amen

August 12

Do You Need to Walk in Wisdom?

Are you trying to make wise decisions? Do you need to know how to respond the way God wants? To find His way for you, seek the kingdom of God first. Be a seeker of His will by following His commandments with a committed heart. What is His will? Ask the Lord to help you determine this as you pray. Then be still and wait for His answers. Set your heart on the things above, where God reigns, and feel His peace. Keep focused on the eternal hope that is yours in Christ to find the wisdom and peace you are seeking!

Dear Lord,

I am focusing on You as I set my heart on Your Word. When I am faithful in prayer and obedient in heart, You will show me much, Lord. There is more in store for me when I wholeheartedly trust You. I will seek the things that are eternal and stop focusing on the things I cannot change in this world. I will keep your commandments so I can walk in wisdom. *"So you shall keep the commandments of the Lord your God by walking in his ways and by fearing him."* Deuteronomy 8:6

In Jesus' Name, Amen

August 13

Where is Your Treasure?

What do You treasure? God wants you to treasure Him. Are you loving the Lord with a devoted heart? There is much in store for You when You trust Him with all Your heart. He wants to bless you with His spiritual blessings. When you keep Him close at heart, the Lord will show You great and mighty things and your faith will increase. When you feel hopeless, cling to the hope of Jesus Christ! He will be Your refuge and strength. Treasure His love for you!

Dear Lord,

Thank You for showing me the way to life as I follow You. I do trust You as I treasure You. I feel Your peace in the stillness of my soul. I feel Your love when I listen with my heart. I will trust You with all my heart instead of trying to figure it all out on my own. Your timing is always perfect as You work all things out for me in Your will and timing! In You, I do find rest for my soul. My heart is with You, Lord! *"Where your treasure is, there your heart will be also,"* Matthew 6:21.

In Jesus' Name, Amen

August 14

Do You Feel the Peace of the Lord?

Are you seeking peace from the storm? Is your heart troubled with the chaos you see around you? Instead of looking at what you cannot change, let the peace of Christ, that is readily available for you, guard your heart and your mind. Jesus gives you His peace when you follow Him. He will take you to His place of peace where you will be free from worry. Surrender all your worries to Him. There is a wonderful plan filled with great promises for you as a child of God. Take His hand and let His peace soothe your soul and calm your heart.

Dear Lord,

Thank You for calming my anxious heart with Your perfect peace that cannot be taken away from me. Even in the midst of trouble, I know Your peace. I keep You close to my heart and my thoughts. You have promised to keep me in perfect peace when I trust in You and Your will. Thank You for infusing my life with Your perfect peace that passes all understanding! It is well with my soul! *"My covenant of peace shall not be removed, says the LORD, who has compassion on you,"* Isaiah 54:10.

In Jesus' Name, Amen

BE STILL

August 15

Are You Walking Humbly Before the Lord?

Are you walking in the darkness of pride? Have you lost your way? Come back home to the love of Christ. He will enlighten you with all hope and joy as you let Him renew your heart. He wants to strengthen you with His mighty power from above. He wants to give you courage for what lies ahead. He will pour His mercy upon you when you humble yourself before Him and ask for forgiveness. Seek mercy and walk humbly before your Lord!

Dear Lord,

Your face shines upon me as I walk humbly before You. My eyes have seen Your glory as I live in Your presence. You have given me renewed hope as I live in Your love. I am bursting with new joy as I let You work in me. Thank You for shining Your light upon me as I serve You with joy in my heart. You are the strength of my soul! I have stepped out of the dark and am living in the light of Your glory! *"Make your face shine upon your servant, and teach me your statutes,"* Psalm 119:135.

In Jesus' Name, Amen

August 16

Are You Afraid to Share Your Heart?

People need love and want to know they are loved. They want to hear good news instead of bad news. Why have we become afraid to speak about what is on our hearts? Have we become silent out of fear or weariness? People need hope and we can speak with positivity when we let our faith shine. Keep speaking about your faith and do not be silent. There are people who need to know the love of Jesus. Stand up for the truth!

Dear Lord,

I know You want me to share love. You desire that I speak about the good news that is found in a relationship with You. As I speak up for truth, Your love sets me free. I do not have to be afraid when You are with me. It is a joy to be in Your presence and it is great to be loved by You. Help me to keep sharing my faith in a way that honors and pleases You, my Lord! *"Do not be afraid, but go on speaking and do not be silent,"* Acts 18:9.

In Jesus' Name, Amen

August 17

Do You Know God's Mercies Never End?

Are you close to the Lord? Is He the Lord of your life? Come closer to His love and let Him speak to your heart. You have been letting other things take priority in your life when the Lord has been wanting you to draw closer to Him. He sees what you are going through and wants to touch you with His love. Believe that His mercies never end. They are new for you every day!

Dear Lord,

Oh, how I love you, Lord! You have been so good to me and I am so thankful for Your love. I know Your love never ends and Your mercies are new every morning. Oh, how great is Your faithfulness to me! Thank You for taking care of me as I let You direct my life. I will keep delighting in You so You can give what You desire for me! *"The steadfast love of the LORD never ceases; his mercies never come to an end; they are new every morning; great is your faithfulness,"* Lamentations 3:22-23.

In Jesus' Name, Amen

August 18

Do You Believe There is Still Hope?

Are you looking for the light at the end of the tunnel? Are you hopeful for what you cannot see but believe is possible? With Christ, all things are possible! He has given you so much to look forward to. You will grow as you go in faith with Him. Walk through the open door before you into new life. Follow His light. There is hope waiting for you. Open your heart and cling to Christ to find eternal life and steadfast love!

Dear Lord,

In my struggles, You are there and ready to save me. When I am lost, You touch my soul and lift me closer to You. As I wander away, You guide me back to You. As I come closer to You, I feel Your love and mercy. As I let go and surrender all to You, my life will be transformed! I am made new in Christ! Thank You for saving me and giving me new life! *"Hear my prayer, O LORD; give ear to my pleas for mercy!"* Psalm 143:1.

In Jesus' Name, Amen

August 19

Who Can You Help?

Does your heart see those who need your prayers? Do your eyes see their needs? Do your ears hear the Lord calling you to help? Are your hands ready to serve? God places people on your heart to reach out and love. He will lead you to the place where He needs you to open your heart. As you serve others, you are serving Him. He is well pleased with you, good and faithful servant.

Dear Lord,

You have called Your people by name to rise and stand firm. You need all of us to reach out and spread love. As I love, I am helping build Your kingdom. There is not one person who does not need love. We were born to love and be loved. Help me to be Your hands and feet and spread Your sweet aroma wherever I go. Your presence has revived my heart and I am ready to go! *"Truly I say to you, as you did it to one of the least of these my brothers, you did it to me,"* Matthew 25:40.

In Jesus' Name, Amen

August 20

Are You Following the Lord Wholeheartedly?

Are you wondering which way to go? Have you looked to the Lord to help you? The world will tell you other ways to go, but the Lord will show you the truth. He wants the best for you, His beloved. When you say yes to Him, you will discover His best plan for you. Trust the Lord with all your heart and do not lean only on your own understanding. In all your ways acknowledge Him, and He will make your path straight!

Dear Lord,

I know You want me to fully trust You. There are some areas of my life I have been holding on to and I need to let go. It is time for me to surrender and let You work all things out for my good and Your glory. Instead of leaving You out, You want me to let You in! I will trust You with all my heart and watch You work all things out even in uncertain, unsettling, and unstable circumstances! *"Yet I wholly followed the LORD my God,"* Joshua 14:8.

In Jesus' Name, Amen

August 21

Are You Worshipping God in Spirit and in Truth?

The Lord wants us to worship Him. He loves our worship in spirit and truth. As we cling to the truth in His Word and let His Spirit come alive in us, we will be true worshippers. The Spirit of the Lord is in those who have given Him their hearts. The truth is found in Jesus Himself. As we spend time in relationship with the Lord, we will find freedom. He has raised us and set us free! Find your freedom in Christ as you freely worship Him!

Dear Lord,

Thank You for giving me all my spiritual blessings. I know You will set me free as I cling tighter to You. I am praising You for all that You have done in me. I have become stronger since You have set me free from sin and given me new life. I am celebrating my freedom as I worship You in spirit and in truth! *"God is spirit, and those who worship him must worship in spirit and truth,"* John 4:24.

In Jesus' Name, Amen

August 22

Why Are You Still Holding Onto Your Concerns?

The Lord wants to help you by taking all your cares and concerns. He loves you and wants to help you. The Lord sees your struggles and setbacks. He has a better plan and is just waiting for you to release all to Him. The Lord is there to catch you when you fall. He will help you, so give Him your burdens. Befriend faith and watch your fears disappear. Take heart and let Jesus touch your heart once again. He is right there with arms wide open. Give Him all your burdens so He can calm your anxious heart.

Dear Lord,

I am letting go of my fears and letting my faith rise. You have promised to help me when I let You in. I will cast all my cares on You so You can help me. You *want* to help me, so I will surrender and give You all my concerns. As I release all my anxieties to You, I am set free at last! *"Casting all your anxieties on him, because he cares for you,"* 1 Peter 5:7.

In Jesus' Name, Amen

August 23

Are You Abiding in the Love of the Lord?

The Lord wants us to abide in His love. He loves us and wants our devotion. When we live in His love, we will be close at heart to Him and will be connected to His heart of love. The love of the Lord remains forever. It is so comforting to know His love never ends and stands eternally! Abide in His love and know the joy of the Lord!

Dear Lord,

Your joy remains in me as I abide in Your love. I will keep growing closer to You while I walk in Your love and live in faith. I know You have promised fullness of joy in Your presence. I will sit at Your feet to be close to You. I want to live in Your presence and under Your influence every day of my life. Right with You is where I feel safe and secure. Thank You for touching me with Your love! My heart is overflowing with joy! *"As the Father has loved me, so have I loved you. Abide in my love,"* John 15:9.

In Jesus' Name, Amen

August 24

Are You Following Christ?

Have you looked to Jesus Christ to give you strength for the challenges ahead of you? Jesus wants to take your hand and pull you to victory! He is a very present help to give you the needed strength and endurance you need for this life. Be an imitator of Christ as you draw closer to His love. Follow His example and come home to the peace and joy that is yours in Christ today!

Dear Lord,

In You, I have been set free! I have everything I need when I come close to You! Thank You for showing me how to live the life You have purposed for me. I am anxious to see what lies ahead as I keep trusting You completely. I will follow You wholeheartedly. In You, I have everything I need! Thank You for giving me new hope in the challenges as I draw closer to Your love! *"Be imitators of me, as I am of Christ,"* 1 Corinthians 11:1.

In Jesus' Name, Amen

August 25

Where Does Your Faith Rest?

God wants us to place our faith in Him. When we look to Him, He will give us wisdom. A little bit of faith will get us a whole lot of hope when we put our trust in God who gives generously. He wants to show us the way as we look to Him, the founder of our faith. We will see with faithful eyes when we open our hearts and believe!

Dear Lord,

You have given me opportunities to grow my faith. I will trust You to lead me where I need to go. I know You are calling me to come closer to You and let my faith in You rise to greater heights. I am believing *You* and not what the world tells me. I will put faith first so You can give me wisdom. I love You, Lord! *"So that your faith might not rest in the wisdom of men, but in the power of God,"* 1 Corinthians 2:5.

In Jesus' Name, Amen

August 26

Are You Giving Love?

Do you know you are loved and are worthy before the King? Do you believe you are forgiven? Jesus Christ, your King, came out of love to love you. He has forgiven you for your sins. He wants you to know His everlasting love. His goodness and kindness will touch your soul when you let Him into your heart. The joy He brings will give you fresh hope. Believe in His love for you and live in eternal love!

Dear Lord,

I know You love me and have forgiven me. I have eternal life because I have believed in Your Son, Jesus Christ! I am living in love as I love You and love others. You want me to share the good news of Your eternal love that saves. It is by grace that I have been saved! I will share this hope as I love You and love other people. Thank You for Your love that never ends! *"For God so loved the world, that he gave his only Son, that whoever believes in him should not perish but have everlasting life,"* John 3:16.

In Jesus' Name, Amen

August 27

Where Are Your Roots?

Are you rooted and grounded in the love of God? Have you let Him grow your faith by trusting Him more? Your Heavenly Father desires for you to firmly plant in the good soil of His Word. When you are planted by God, you will not be uprooted when problems come. Circumstances cannot take you away from the love of the Lord. You will grow stronger as you face challenges that come your way. When you are planted by God's love, you will be secure and stable. Let God plant you in good soil so you can bloom!

Dear Lord,

Oh, how I love knowing that once You plant me, strong roots will grow deep. The soil of my heart longs for Your nourishment. I grow stronger as You plant me deeper. These challenges I am facing are making me grow deeper roots. Thank You for putting Your Word in my heart and Your Spirit in my soul. I will keep growing closer to You as I live planted in Your amazing love! *"Every plant that my heavenly Father has not planted will be rooted up,"* Matthew 15:13.

In Jesus' Name, Amen

August 28

Do the Words of Your Mouth Bless Others?

Have you asked for the Lord to guard your mouth before you speak? Have you stopped to pray before you let words come from your lips? God will help you as you speak. He wants words of love and encouragement to flow from your lips. The world needs more love, and you can be that light. Start today by seeking the Lord's guidance before you say what is on your mind. As you set your mind on the Spirit, the words that flow out of your mouth will bless others!

Dear Lord,

Thank You for guarding my heart and my mind! I want to bless others with words of affirmation. In this world I will face many problems, but You, O Lord, will help me anytime I need You. You are the light that guides me into truth. You help me see the good around me. I need You, Lord, to guide my speech. I want to bless others with kind and loving words. *"Set a guard, O LORD, over my mouth; keep watch over the door of my lips!"* Psalm 141:3.

In Jesus' Name, Amen

August 29

Are You Feeling Faint?

Are you feeling faint and weak? Do you need more strength? God wants to strengthen you and help you in your weakness. He wants to be your perfect peace. When you let Christ in, He will attend to your needs. He wants to help you. Turn towards the one who will give you all that you need. Strength and healing are possible through Jesus Christ!

Dear Lord,

You are my perfect peace. I have found healing in You as Your presence is an open door to restoration. I am walking through Your door as I trust You more each day. I know You will attend to the voice of my prayers as I lift my requests to You. I am looking to You for extra strength and healing. Give me added strength, power, and endurance as I embrace You! *"He gives power to the faint, and to him who has no might he increases strength,"* Isaiah 40:29.

In Jesus' Name, Amen

August 30

Do You Believe You Are Loved?

Do you believe God loves you? Have you asked Him to be the Lord of your life? If so, is God your *first* love? He loves you and wants you to know His steadfast, enduring love. He wants you to love Him by putting Him first in your life. The Lord, your God, is faithful and patient towards you. He loves you and has forgiven you. Feel His love and follow Him faithfully!

Dear Lord,

Thank You for loving me! I am blessed to know Your enduring love and amazing grace. I believe in love because I know You love me. You sacrificed Your only begotten Son so that all would be saved from sin and know the power of Your love. Your love has saved me! I am free to be who You made me to be because I am loved and saved by Your grace! "*God is love,*" 1 John 4:8.

In Jesus' Name, Amen

August 31

Are You Remaining Faithful
with Steadfast Purpose?

Have you lost your faith? Are you working with purpose for the Lord? The Lord needs you and wants to see your faith. He knows what you are facing and wants to help you. Keep walking with steadfast purpose and the Lord will give you renewed hope. He is working even when you cannot see. There is assurance of what you hope for in the Lord. Keep the faith. Stay faith-filled and let the peace of Christ rule in your heart! When you live out what you believe, you will experience His blessings. The Lord is always faithful to you!

Dear Lord,

I am clinging to You by faith. I see what You need me to do and I am blessed as I keep moving forward. I will keep my faith first. I will not let fear keep me from living out Your purpose for me. When I stay faithful, I will see all You have promised me. My faith has come alive as I live out what I believe! *"Remain faithful to the Lord with steadfast purpose,"* Acts 11:23.

In Jesus' Name, Amen

Monthly Reflections

As you pray and lean on the Lord's promises, write what the Lord has revealed to you for this month.

Have I not
commanded you?
Be strong
AND COURAGEOUS.
Do not be frightened,
and do not be dismayed,
FOR THE LORD
YOUR GOD
is with you
WHEREVER YOU
GO.
JOSHUA 1:9

September 1

Do You Hear the Word of God?

Do you hear the word of God? Are you obeying what God says? His commands are not burdensome, but instead, are for your own good. When you listen and obey Him, you will be blessed. Every good and perfect gift comes from above where Jesus is sitting at the right hand of the Father. Seek Jesus and find eternal gifts. Your blessings will come when you trust and obey the Lord in all your ways! It is not too late to come back! Grace is yours in Christ Jesus.

Dear Lord,

Thank You for calling me. I will be still, listen, and obey You faithfully. My heart is open to trust You more with each new day. Living in Your blessings is the way I want to live. I need You, Lord, all the time. Your prescription for peace is in Your presence. I will draw closer to You so You can fill me with peace. Blessings and peace abound in Your loving arms! *"Blessed rather are those who hear the word of God and keep it!"* Luke 11:28.

In Jesus' Name, Amen

September 2

Are You Waiting on the Lord?

When is the last time we have waited in silence for the Lord and praised Him for all He has done? He wants us to thank Him for the answers to prayers. He yearns for our praise. His glory reigns in and around us. He speaks even in the silence. When we listen, He shows us much in the waiting as we lift our hearts in praise and worship. Rejoice in the Lord, again, rejoice as you wait!

Dear Lord,

I am thankful for Your abundant blessings! I love You so much and want to show You by my actions. I will press on by faith and let go of my fear. I know You are there even in the silence. You are my salvation. As I am still, I know You are God. You have opened the door to my heart and helped me see new opportunities. I will walk faithfully with You through the open door no man can shut! Hallelujah! *"For God alone my soul waits in silence; from him comes my salvation,"* Psalm 62:1.

In Jesus' Name, Amen

September 3

Are You Doing the Will of God?

We all have choices about what we say and do. We know God's law, but are we delighting to do what He has commanded us to do? Are we obeying what the Lord asks of us? His will is best for us. He has given us direction, but are we walking in His will and His way? His way is love. His way is forgiveness. His way is peace. His way is the only way to life! Turn around and begin walking on the path of freedom with Christ! He is your way-maker!

Dear Lord,

I know there will be trouble in this world. When I take my eyes off You, Lord, I tend to focus more on my problems. But You are God and are bigger than any circumstance I will ever face! You give me new hope as I cling to You and Your promises. I delight to do Your will and I will walk in Your ways. I am leaning on You as I trust and obey You, my Lord! *"I desire to do your will, O my God; your law is within my heart,"* Psalm 40:8.

In Jesus' Name, Amen

September 4

Is Your Soul Thirsting for God?

God wants us to thirst for Him. He is a living God ready to meet our needs as we come to Him. He yearns for us to take His hand and walk to freedom. He will find us when we open our hearts to Him. He is a living God full of hope for us. As we live one moment at a time, we will be blessed by His presence. Are you thirsty for God? Do you have needs you want God to supply? He knows what you need even before you ask. He is open to your requests and ready to bless you. Thirst for the living God and let Him bless you richly with living hope each day.

Dear Lord,

My soul yearns for You. I am thirsting for You. I am hungry for You. I know You will supply all my needs as I humbly come to You in prayer. Thank You for showing me Your glory as You light up the sky with the light of Your love! I love You! *"My soul thirsts for God, for the living God,"* Psalm 42:2.

In Jesus' Name, Amen

September 5

Are You Living Out Your Love?

We all have opportunities to love. God has given each of us His truth so we can live in love. He wants us to live in truth by living out our faith. Have you just talked about your faith? Are you living it out? Have you put feet to your faith? Jesus needs you to step out of your comfort zone and serve. It pleases the Lord to see your faith. He will bless you when you walk closely with Him by obeying His truth. He can do more in you than you can ever imagine if you step out in love. His power will come to your life when you activate the power of Christ in you!

Dear Lord,

I know You are going to do more in me as I step out in faith and act in truth and deed. Words have meaning when they are combined with actions. I will strive to live out what I believe by serving You. There is more in store for me when I trust and obey! *"Little children, let us not love in word or talk but in deed and in truth,"* 1 John 3:18.

In Jesus' Name, Amen

September 6

Do You Need an Infusion of Strength?

Are you feeling weak? Do you need to be infused with strength? God has given you grace so you can find strength in Him. When you believe in Jesus Christ as your personal Savior, God puts His Spirit inside you. Activate the Spirit of God in you by surrendering to His will. He will do something new in you when you let go of your old self and put on the Spirit of God. Seek His presence. He is calling you into a devoted and deeper relationship with Him. You will grow stronger when you let go and let God cover you with His grace and love!

Dear Lord,

You want me to be devoted to You. As I grow in grace, You will strengthen me with Your power and give me purpose. I know You are calling me into a deeper relationship with You. I feel Your strength in my weakness. When I am weak, You are strong. Thank You for attending to the voice of my prayers as I lift my heart to You. Help me to live in grace. *"My grace is sufficient for you, for my power is made perfect in weakness,"* 2 Corinthians 12:9.

In Jesus' Name, Amen

September 7

How is Your Endurance?

Are you keeping your head up and your heart close to God? Are you determined not to give up the good fight of the faith? The one who endures to the end will be saved. Keep walking faithfully and God will infuse you with His great power, the Holy Spirit. The Spirit of God is close to you, faithful one. He will energize you with vitality and strength as you keep moving forward. Look up and see the promises of the Lord!

Dear Lord,

I am full of hope as I keep walking faithfully one step at a time. My obedience to You will keep me on the right track. I am full of faith as I trust You to show me the way. I will not give up or get discouraged as You guide me and as I lean on You. Everything is going to be alright as I cling tighter to You. *"But the one who endures to the end will be saved,"* Matthew 24:13.

In Jesus' Name, Amen

September 8

Are You Looking Up?

God gives you gifts to receive. Receive them with joy. His gifts are perfect and good and come down from Him, the Father of lights. Look up to see His gifts that He wants to give you. Open your heart to receive all God wants to give you. He has wonders far above He wants you to enjoy for His glory! Ask and you shall receive every perfect gift from above!

Dear Lord,

Thank You for putting Your Spirit within me when I have believed. Your joy has touched every part of me. I am breathing in Your love that has touched all the places of my heart and my soul. I am alive with hope as I experience Your perfect peace that enriches my soul. Thank you, Lord, for every good and perfect gift! I love You! *"Every good gift and every perfect gift is from above…"* James 1:17.

In Jesus' Name, Amen

September 9

Are You Putting Feet to Your Faith?

Do you have faith? Are you working out your faith with fear and trembling? God wants you to be faithful to Him by obeying Him. He has works in mind for you. Your faith will grow when you live out what you believe for God. He is watching you make choices each day. He is looking to see what you will do. Show the Lord how much you love Him by putting Him first and obeying what He has put on your heart to do.

Dear Lord,

I will live out my faith by obeying Your commands. I know You have good works for me to do. *I will listen and go.* You have called me to a higher purpose. Thank You for showing me how to live out what I believe. My faith comes alive when I work for *You*, Lord. Speak, Lord, for Your servant is listening! *"So also faith by itself, if it does not have works, is dead,"* James 2:17.

In Jesus' Name, Amen

September 10

Is Your Heart Turned Towards God?

Is your heart full of the peace of Christ? Have you struggled because there seems to be no peace around you? In this world you will have trouble, but take heart, because Christ has come to give you peace. His presence will turn your sadness into peace. Perfect peace is not the absence of problems, but the presence of Christ in the midst of problems. Where God reigns, there is righteousness. A harvest of righteousness is sown in peace. Be a peacemaker for the Lord. Come closer to Christ and feel His peace!

Dear Lord,

Thank You for giving me peace. I am close to You and I feel Your peace inside me. Your peace rules in my heart because I have made You Lord of my life. Thank You for touching me with Your peace. I am right where You want me to be—in Your presence! *"And a harvest of righteousness is sown in peace by those who make peace,"* James 3:18.

In Jesus' Name, Amen

September 11

Do You Need to Get Back on Your Feet?

Are you needing help getting back on your feet? Have you looked to the Lord to help you rise? The Lord your God will be your strength and your song. He will give you hope just when you need Him. He is only a prayer away from giving you the strength you need. Let Him touch your heart. He will comfort and protect you. He is waiting to bless you with an extra measure of strength for what lies ahead! Look up and let go to revive your heart and renew your soul!

Dear Lord,

I can do all things through You, Lord God, who strengthens me. When I need help, You are there. When I am weak, You promise to lift me up. All I need to do is call Your name, let go of my old self, and cling to You. I have new life because You are my strength. I am resting in Your love and protection with added strength in my inner being! It is well with my soul! *"The LORD GOD is my strength and my song,"* Isaiah 12:2.

In Jesus' Name, Amen

September 12

Are you Choosing the Perfect Peace of Christ?

Are you trusting the Lord to give you His peace? Have you set your mind on the Spirit where peace reigns? You have a choice about where you set your mind and how you live your life. Christ wants you to trust Him. He has perfect peace waiting for you when you trust Him completely. There are many ways you can go, but only one way that leads to peace. Choose the way to peace, Jesus Christ!

Dear Lord,

I will set my mind on You to find perfect peace. There is peace waiting for me when I draw closer to You. As I put You in the center of my life, I am farther away from the things that take me away from peace. I discover peace when I cling to You, my Lord. Your peace settles my restlessness and comforts me. Peace be still my soul! *"You keep him in perfect peace whose mind is stayed on you, because he trusts in you,"* Isaiah 26:3.

In Jesus' Name, Amen

September 13

Are You Listening to the Lord?

Are you hearing what God is asking you to do? Have you been obeying the promptings of the Holy Spirit? God has called you to come closer to His love. He wants to give you His instructions for your journey. He has put His Spirit inside You so You can have His power and be infused with His strength. He needs you to faithfully obey what He has asked. Come closer to His love and be filled with the power of the Holy Spirit who will guide you to live the life God has planned for you. He is watching you and wants to find you obedient, beloved child of God.

Dear Lord,

I know You want me to listen to You so You can lead and direct me. I will faithfully follow You where You lead me. It is so good to know Your love. I am eagerly awaiting Your direction so I can follow You where You lead me. My heart is overflowing with hope as I faithfully obey and follow You! *"For the eyes of the Lord are on the righteous, and his ears are open to their prayer…"* 1 Peter 3:12.

In Jesus' Name, Amen

September 14

Are You Letting Your Love Flow?

God loves us so much that He has given us His Son. Whoever believes in Jesus Christ will have everlasting life. His love *saves*. His love *renews*. His love *heals*. His love brings *hope* and *peace*. His love *never ends*! Help us Lord to love others from a pure heart of love as You have loved us. We need You, Lord, because these days are challenging for us. Touch our hearts with Your restoring and redeeming love!

Dear Lord,

Oh, how I love You, Lord. You have given me a new heart and put a new spirit within me. I am living out my faith by letting Your love work inside me. I will keep serving because You have called me to serve. I will press on to new opportunities to live out what I believe. I will live in Your steadfast love! *"Love one another earnestly from a pure heart,"* 1 Peter 1:22.

In Jesus' Name, Amen

September 15

Have You Considered All God Has Done for You?

What do You treasure? Are you loving the Lord with a devoted heart? God wants you to treasure Him. He yearns for your devoted heart. Trust Him with all Your heart. When you keep Him close at heart, the Lord will show You great and mighty things and your faith will increase. Cling to the hope of Jesus Christ! Treasure His love for you and consider all He has done for you!

Dear Lord,

Thank You for showing me the way to life when I follow You. When I trust You, there is much in store for me. I know Your love as I listen with my heart. I will trust You with all my heart instead of trying to figure everything out on my own. Your timing is perfect. You work all things out for me in Your perfect will and timing! In You, I find rest for my soul. My heart is with You, Lord! *"Only fear the LORD and serve him faithfully with all your heart. For consider what great things he has done for you,"* 1 Samuel 12:24.

In Jesus' Name, Amen

September 16

Are You Carrying Burdens?

Do you have burdens you are carrying and weighing you down? Have you felt what feels like the weight of the world on your shoulders? When you cast your burdens onto the Lord, He will help you by lightening your load. In Psalm 55:22, there is hope as you read truth. *"Cast your burden on the LORD, and he will sustain you."* Listen to this Word from the Lord so He can sustain you. You are struggling and have not looked up to the living hope found in Jesus Christ. You are giving in to the frustrations and fears from the world. Step back from the world and its ways and see the victory that is yours in the arms of your Savior! He will sustain you so that you can live victoriously!

Dear Lord,

I will let go of my burdens one at a time. I have been trying to control my situations by carrying all my burdens and the burdens of other people. You have offered a way out through my faith in You. I will take Your hand and let You help me. You will take my burdens.

In Jesus' Name, Amen

September 17

Have You Opened Your Heart to the Steadfast Love of the Lord?

Are you searching for love? God's love for you is real. He truly loves you and wants your heart. Every moment you open your heart to more of Him brings you closer to His love. He yearns for your devotion. Come back to the one who is devoted to you. His love is steadfast and cannot be shaken. Open your heart to faith and let the Lord love you. Believe and repeat His promise for you in Psalm 57:10, *"For your steadfast love is great to the heavens, your faithfulness to the clouds."*

Dear Lord,

Your love amazes me! I can make a mistake, and You still love me. I can turn away for a while and You take me back and shelter me in Your arms of love. I will look to You for my needs as I believe in You and Your promises to me. I love You. My heart is filled with joy and peace, and I have this hope deep in my soul that cannot be explained. I hear You calling my name and telling me, "I love you, dear child of mine!"

In Jesus' Name, Amen

September 18

Do You Want to be Well?

Are you praying for good health in body, mind, and soul? God hears your prayers. He will hear you when you ask Him for what you need. God wants to help you, and those you are praying for, to be in good health in body, mind, and soul. He knows your requests are made from your heart and will answer you. He rewards those who pray in faith believing He will answer their prayers. God is listening to your faithful prayers and He wants to see you and those on your heart be made well. *""For I will restore health to you, and your wounds I will heal," declares the LORD..."* Jeremiah 30:17.

Dear Lord,

I know You will attend to the voice of my prayers. I have multiple people I am praying for. Hear my prayers, O Lord, and touch us with Your mighty hand and give us healing and wholeness. This world has pulled us away from You. We are restless, discontent, and stressed. Bring us back to You. I need You, Lord!

In Jesus' Name, Amen

September 19

Do You Know the Joy of the Lord?

God sees your tears. He weeps with you when you cry. He feels your pain and wants to comfort you. God promises joy will come even through the tears. He promises to be the joy and the strength of your soul. When you are weak, He will be your strength. You can find joy even in your weakness when you have God present in your life. When you say, "I can't." God says, "You can, dear one, with me." Be present in God's presence. Take hold of His hand and believe He can do more inside you through the power of the Holy Spirit! Let the joy of the Lord come alive in you! *"Weeping may tarry for the night, but joy comes with the morning,"* Psalm 30:5.

Dear Lord,

Thank You for Your promises that never end. Your promise of joy is real, and I believe what You say. I know there is an abundance of joy where You are, so I will faithfully keep following You! In your presence, there is fullness of joy! I choose joy!

In Jesus' Name, Amen

September 20

Why Are You Afraid?

God is your light and your salvation. He is the light that will open your eyes to see in the dark. When you are afraid, God will help you out of the dark and into the light. There is no fear with Christ inside you because nothing can come between you and His light of hope. Have you drawn to fear or faith? Fear is the opposite of faith. When you are afraid, you will make decisions that are not in the will of God. But when you have faith, your fear will disappear. The power of God will work mightily in you. Faith or fear? Which will you let rule in you? *"The LORD is my light and my salvation, whom shall I fear?"* Psalm 27:1.

Dear Lord,

There is no need to fear when I put my trust in You. Even when I cannot see, You will open my eyes to the truth in love. With You, there is nothing to fear because I have perfect peace in Your presence. Thank You for opening my eyes and helping me navigate the darkness around me. I am putting faith over fear!

In Jesus' Name, Amen

September 21

Are You Looking for God's Path to Peace?

God will show you the way to peace. He knows the path that will lead you there. He wants you to walk in it. He knows the way you should go. Are you ready to let Him show you the way? Will you surrender all to God? He wants the best for you. Let go of all bitterness and offense you have been holding onto and let God fill your heart with His peace. His perfect peace will comfort you and renew your soul! *"Make me to know Your ways, O LORD; teach me your paths,"* Psalm 25:4.

Dear Lord,

Thank You for calming my soul. I am comforted by Your peace. I know You attend to the voice of my prayers as I lift my requests to You. As I humble myself before You, I hear Your soothing voice calling me to come back to Your peace. You want me to live and love in perfect peace even among the unrest in the world. In this world there is trouble, but I will take heart knowing You, O Lord, will show me the way to peace in Your presence!

In Jesus' Name, Amen

September 22

Have You Called Upon the Lord For His Guidance?

The Lord is near to you. He has much to tell and show you. Call upon Him and He will answer your prayers. There are deep and hidden things only He knows. He will show you when you let Him in. Are you eager to know His plan for you? Let Him show you the way. Keep the faith and watch the Lord move for you. He will guide you into all truth when you call upon Him by faith. *"He reveals deep and hidden things; he knows what is in the darkness, and the light dwells with him,"* Daniel 2:22.

Dear Lord,

You will listen when I call upon You. I am just a prayer away from Your grace and guidance. There is hope in the waiting and my faith is strengthened as I listen. Help me to see You in the waiting. As I wait, I will trust You more because my heart is ready to receive all from You! You will show me all the blessings that are mine in You. I have found all I need in Your promises!

In Jesus' Name, Amen

September 23

Are You Counting Your Blessings?

We all have blessings to count and recount. God has given us all so much to be grateful for. Let us all give thanks for our God who is good *all* the time! His mercies never end and are new each morning. Great is His faithfulness! Have you praised God today for His goodness and grace? Instead of worrying, keep praising God from whom all blessings flow! You are blessed by the grace of God, indeed! Blessed be the name of the Lord, our God! *"I will give thanks to the LORD with my whole heart; I will recount all of your wonderful deeds,"* Psalm 9:1.

Dear Lord,

You are so amazing, Lord! I thank You for all Your goodness and grace. Your amazing grace covers me and I am so thankful for Your many blessings! I see the light of Your love that covers and secures me. Thank You for loving me so faithfully. Great is Your faithfulness! I give You honor and praise as I recount all my wonderful blessings!

In Jesus' Name, Amen

September 24

Do You Believe Nothing
is too Hard for God?

God knows your struggles and your worries. He understands your pain and sees your heart has been broken. His outstretched arms are open for you. There is nothing He cannot do! Have you asked for what is on your heart? Open your heart and let the Lord speak to you. He wants you to seek Him and the things above where He has spiritual blessings waiting for you. Look up and find your treasure where His heart is. Where is your heart? *"Nothing is too hard for you,"* Jeremiah 32:17.

Dear Lord,

I believe nothing is too hard for You! I know You want what is best for me. You ask that I trust You. It is time for me to let go completely of things that weigh me down so You can do Your work in me. I have been trying to make things happen on my own without Your outstretched arms holding me up. Instead of keeping my eyes on the problems, You want me to adjust my focus to be completely on You.

In Jesus' Name, Amen

September 25

Do You Believe God is Always Faithful?

Not all have faith or believe. Some have a little faith at times but go back to doubting when life becomes tough. Others struggle to believe at all, unless they see it with their own eyes. Faith is being sure of what you hope for and certain of what you cannot see. When faith rises over fear, we let our belief and trust in God rule in our hearts and we see with new spiritual vision. To walk in faith, you will believe even when you do not see. Open your eyes and see God is always faithful! *"For not all have faith. But the Lord is faithful…"* 2 Thessalonians 3:2-3.

Dear Lord,

You want me to keep walking in faith even when I cannot see the details. I will put one foot in front of the other and go the direction You are taking me. You are faithful to me even when my unbelief starts to creep into my life. Help me with the unbelief You see in me! I will let my faith increase. I will keep You close to my heart. Even in these uncertain times You are always faithful!

In Jesus' Name, Amen

September 26

Do You Believe God's Power
Can Do More in You?

God wants to work in you for His will to come to life. He will work all things out for your good and His glory. He has given you the power of the Holy Spirit when you believed in His Son, Jesus Christ, as your personal Savior. He can transform you. Are you ready to surrender all so God can work in your life and your heart? Let go and let God do His work. He will do abundantly more in you than you could ever dream or imagine! *"Now to him who is able to do far more abundantly than all we ask or think, according to the power at work within us,"* Ephesians *3:20.*

Dear Lord,

I know You are working in me so Your glory shines in my life! I am so excited I know Your power lives inside of me. I have activated this power of the Holy Spirit in my life by believing in Your Son and Your Word. You have brought me hope. I surrender all to You! I trust You for all I need and more. I am letting Your glory shine and reign in me! I do believe!

In Jesus' Name, Amen

September 27

How Will You Respond to Others?

We all have an opportunity to respond with kindness. Even when others try to provoke us to anger, God wants us to respond with a soft and gentle answer. He knows how we can be challenged at times, but with God helping us, we can speak with love and hope. Instead of quenching the Spirit, our words of kindness will bring life and peace. Encourage others with gentleness and let your words bless others! *"A soft answer turns away wrath, but a harsh word stirs up anger,"* Proverbs 15:1.

Dear Lord,

I want to live in peace. To do that, I must watch how I respond to others. My words can either bring peace or stir up conflict. It is Your will, Lord, that I guard my heart and my mouth so that what flows from both will honor You. Your desire is for us to live peacefully with each other and treat each other with respect. Help me to respond with love and grace even when I am challenged. I will defend my faith by responding with kindness, goodness, gentleness, and love.

In Jesus' Name, Amen

September 28

Are You Seeking God?

There is a God in heaven who reveals mysteries. He is waiting for you to seek Him so He can reveal much to you. When you search for Him, you will find Him. He is waiting for you to spend time with Him because He desires a relationship with you. Have you made time for God? He has much to show you. Give Him your heart. Open your heart and let His love reign in yours! *"Making known to us the mystery of his will, according to his purpose..."* Ephesians 1:9.

Dear Lord,

I believe You will open the door for me and show me where You want me to go. You have a greater plan for me that I will see when I step out of my comfort zone and step through the door You open for me. No man can stop what You have ordained. You will reveal much to me as I keep trusting You. My life is in Your loving hands, Lord! I will keep my faith as I walk closely with You and see Your wonderful mysteries revealed in my life!

In Jesus' Name, Amen

September 29

Are You Devoting Yourself to Prayer?

Are you devoted to God in prayer? Will you join with others and lift your heart to God? He listens as you pray. God wants us to pray together in one accord. He sees our devotion and knows our hearts. When two or more join together to lift their hearts up in prayer, God is among them. He listens and will answer their dedicated prayers. Have you continued to pray and asked the Lord for what you need? He is listening closely and will answer you as you faithfully pray! It is time to pray! *"All these with one accord were devoting themselves to prayer..."* Acts 1:14.

Dear Lord,

I know You hear me when I pray. I believe You will answer my requests in Your will, in Your timing, and for Your glory. I will keep on praying and seeking You, my Lord! You are faithful to answer me and those who pray. Your answers are but a prayer away! Thank You, Lord, for making Your presence known to us as we pray together in one accord and with one heart devoted to You!

In Jesus' Name, Amen

September 30

Are You in Awe of God's Wonders?

God has numerous wonders for you to behold. Have you noticed His glory and power around you? He has shown you His glory in the heavens above. What about in your life? He gave you His power, in the gift of the Holy Spirit, when you believed in Jesus Christ as your Savior. This new spirit inside you envelopes you in God's love. Blessings abound for you when you trust Him. Let His power come to life in You now. Fully activate the power of the Holy Spirit in your life. He can do more inside you when you let Him work powerfully in you! Are you ready for awe to come to your soul? *"Awe came upon every soul..."* Acts 2:43.

Dear Lord,

You are so wonderful and powerful, Lord! I am in awe of You and the wonders You show me. When I believed, Your power activated inside me. You give me renewed hope and ordained work in my life as I keep trusting You. I will keep believing and praying with confidence and power from the Holy Spirit. My soul is rejoicing and in awe of You, Lord!

In Jesus' Name, Amen

Monthly Reflections

As you pray and lean on the Lord's promises, write what the Lord has revealed to you for this month.

THEREFORE,
IF ANYONE IS
in Christ,
HE IS
a new creation.
The old has
passed away;
Behold,
THE NEW HAS
COME.
2 CORINTHIANS 5:17

October 1

Are You Wanting to be Free from Sin?

God's forgiveness is for all who believe in Jesus and confess their sins. When you repent and turn from sin, there is new life in Christ! Your old self dies when you receive Christ. He creates new life in you as He puts His Spirit inside you. Are you living in the power of the Holy Spirit given to you? Turn again and activate the power of Christ by living out your faith and setting your mind on the Spirit. There is freedom from sin when you put away self and take hold of the Spirit! *"Repent therefore, and turn back, that your sins may be blotted out,"* Acts 3:19.

Dear Lord,

I know I have freedom in You, Lord, because I have asked You to be my Savior. And because I have believed in You with all my heart and confessed my sins to You, I have been given new life in Christ. I will not let sin separate me from You as return to You and live in the power of the Holy Spirit with the joy of my salvation. If the Son sets me free, I will be free, indeed!

In Jesus' Name, Amen

October 2

Are You Obeying God?

God wants our obedience. When we obey Him, we are showing God that we love Him. Have you listened to His commands? Are you following them? Are you obeying God rather than men? God needs you to step out and make a difference for Him by letting go of your fear. You have let others control your thoughts and hold you down. Christ wants to lift you up as you trust Him more and more. He will exalt you at the proper time when you humble yourself before Him. Stop listening to the other voices and let God's voice be the one you hear and obey to find freedom and peace! *"We must obey God rather than men,"* Acts 5:29.

Dear Lord,

You will never lead me in the wrong direction when I trust in You. I have seen Your glory. I will stay close to You. I am prepared for more opportunities to share Your love. I am listening to what You need me to do, Lord. You want me to be a witness so that others may see You. I will not let anything or anyone else stop me from pursuing You with all my heart!

In Jesus' Name, Amen

October 3

Are You Devoted to Prayer and the Ministry of the Word?

God wants us to pray, read, and mediate upon His Word. He hears our prayers. He knows what we need each moment. The Lord is so good to us. *All the time*. And He is working even when we cannot see. Lift your hands and your hearts to Him so He can help you as you pray and read His promises. He wants you to respond to His promises for you. So, open your heart wide and let Him fill it. Be devoted to the Lord so His promises will come to life in You! *"But we will devote ourselves to prayer and to the ministry of the word,"* Acts 6:4.

Dear Lord,

I hear Your comforting words as I pray. I am listening to Your heart as I give You mine. Your promises have touched my heart and my soul. It is so good to pray and read Your promises to me! Thank You for touching my soul with Your love and power. I am strengthened as I keep believing Your promises for me. I am fully devoted to You!

In Jesus' Name, Amen

October 4

Are You Ready to See Joy in Your City?

Is it possible to have joy where you dwell? There is hope for joy when people live and dwell in unity and love. We may not agree, but we can come together to pray and praise the Lord for His never-ending love and grace. The joy of the Lord comes when He lives in our hearts. With the Lord in focus, we see things from His perspective. The desires of our hearts change when the Lord is the center of our lives. Looking for joy in your city? What have you done to make a difference right where you live? The Lord needs you to dwell in His love and be a beacon of light to shine His love into the hearts of those around you! *"So there was much joy in that city,"* Acts 8:8.

Dear Lord,

There is hope for joy when I do my part to spread Your love to those around me. I want to see joy in my city! As I pray for my city, I believe joy is possible. There is revival for those who love and dwell in unity! Let there be joy in my city!

In Jesus' Name, Amen

October 5

Do You Want to be Healed?

Jesus Christ will heal you. He wants to make you whole. Ask Him for healing and believe He will. Take his hand and let Him strengthen you. He will completely heal your body, mind, and soul when you surrender and let Him work in you. Are you praying for healing? Have you reached out to Jesus and waited patiently for His healing? Believe in the healing power of Jesus Christ, rise, and walk victoriously! *"Jesus Christ heals you; rise and make your bed,"* Acts 9:34.

Dear Lord,

I *believe* you heal, and I will keep praying for Your healing for myself and others on my heart. I *know* you heal in Your will and in Your timing and for Your glory! I have seen miracles when You have healed so many people, Lord! You have touched the hearts of the heartbroken with Your healing hands. You have given new life to those who were dead in spirit. We will faithfully keep praying for healing in the name of Jesus Christ! We will rise together, healed and whole, through the power of Jesus Christ!

In Jesus' Name, Amen

October 6

Do You Know the Holy Spirit?

The Holy Spirit will breathe life and power into each person who surrenders to Him. He is a powerful life-giving Spirit who guides you into all truth. He speaks to your heart in a way that gives you deeper understanding of His Word. When you activate His power, you see a remarkable difference in the way you see people and problems. He gives you inner joy and peace that sets your heart on fire with passion and purpose. Are you ready to be filled with the Holy Spirit? Look up, listen, and obey to receive all that is yours in Christ Jesus! *"The Holy Spirit fell on all who heard the word,"* Acts 10:44.

Dear Lord,
I believe You, Lord, have empowered me with life and freedom as I live by the heartbeat of the Holy Spirit. I listened and surrendered to You. Your power has come to life in me in a new way. My old self has gone and my new self was born in You the day I felt Your touch in me. Thank You for touching my life!
In Jesus' Name, Amen

October 7

Are You Listening to God Through His Word?

God shows us treasures in His Word. When we read it and pray for understanding, He speaks through each word that is alive with the breath of His Spirit. When we listen, He gives us guidance. When we trust, He enriches our lives with spiritual blessings. When we obey, He blesses our lives with peace and joy. Open your Bible to the messages within and God will speak to you. The Holy Spirit comes alive in His Word. Live out the truths within and find contentment. *"But the word of God increased and multiplied,"* Acts 12:24.

Dear Lord,

Thank You for Your Word that is sharper than a two-edged sword. Your Word gives me life as it increases and multiplies in my life. I love hearing You speak to me through Your Word. As I live out what You have written to me, I am enriched in every way! I am listening to You and I will spread Your hope through the gospel written on my heart!

In Jesus' Name, Amen

October 8

Are You Filled with the
Joy of the Holy Spirit?

The Holy Spirit promises us joy! When we wait for the promised Holy Spirit and let Him come alive inside us, He will fill us with utmost joy! This new life is ours as we choose to live a Spirit-filled life. He always strengthens us for what lies ahead when we trust and obey Him. He listens, loves, and cares for you. Hear the Spirit calling you to be enriched in every way as you seek His way! *"And the disciples were filled with joy and with the Holy Spirit,"* Acts 13:52.

Dear Lord,

Thank You for enriching my life with utmost joy and the power of the Holy Spirit working inside of me! I am full of the joy of the Holy Spirit when I live surrendered to You. I am living with Your power working in me which gives me confidence, hope, security, and wisdom. To live in the Spirit is life and peace. I will trust and obey Your promptings for me so I can continue to walk this path to freedom in the Spirit. Where the Spirit of the Lord is, there is joy!

In Jesus' Name, Amen

October 9

Are You Speaking Boldly for the Lord?

We all have opportunities to be bolder in our faith. We can make a difference as we share the good news of our hope that is found in Jesus Christ. People today are struggling and have no hope. They are holding on by a thread and need someone to speak and act in love and truth. When we boldly share our faith, it can help others to know the hope that can be found in Jesus. He is the way to truth and life! Share hope today and bring Jesus to those who need you to be bold. Remain faithful and proclaim His excellencies! *"So they remained for a long time, speaking boldly for the Lord…"* Acts 14:3.

Dear Lord,

I want to continue to speak and act boldly for You, Lord. My hope is found in You and I want to share this hope with others. Help me be stronger and braver as I continue to stand firm in my faith. There is an urgency in my soul to keep sharing Your light as the days grow darker. You want all to come to repentance and seek You with their whole hearts.

In Jesus' Name, Amen

October 10

Do You Want the Gift of the Holy Spirit?

The Lord will give you the gift of the Holy Spirit when you give Him your heart and believe in Jesus Christ as your personal Savior. You shall be His witnesses of love and truth as you tune into the Holy Spirit's frequency. His truth will set you free. Live in His power. Have you received your special gift? Open your heart, tune into His frequency, and let the Holy Spirit come alive in you! *"And God, who knows the heart, bore witness to them, by giving them the Holy Spirit just as He did to us,"* Acts 15:8.

Dear Lord,

I am grateful for the special gift of the Holy Spirit which is actively working in me. When I need guidance, You teach me. When I need to know truth, You give me wisdom. When I need a friend, You comfort me. When I need strength, You strengthen me. When I need hope, You direct my heart to Your love. I am empowered with the Holy Spirit and blessed by Your constant presence in my life, Lord. I am so grateful and humbled for Your endless love through the power and presence of the Holy Spirit!

In Jesus' Name, Amen

October 11

Do You Believe that God can do Miracles?

Do you believe in miracles? Ordinary people with great faith in God have seen miracles in their lives. Their faith has given them renewed hope as they trust God and believe all things are possible with Him. It is God who works all things out for good for those who love Him and are called according to His purpose. You are God's miracle. He made you perfect in His image when He knit you in your mother's womb. He wants you, His miracle, to live with the Holy Spirit active inside you. He has called you to pray in the Spirit with power and believe when you pray for revival of your heart. It is time to pray and believe in the extraordinary miracles of God! *"And God was doing extraordinary miracles..."* Acts19:11.

Dear Lord,

Thank You for showing me Your miracles. I do believe You have extraordinary miracles for me to experience. I have already seen things happen that no man can explain away. Your miracles abound! I will continue praying. I believe You will do great things in and through me as I keep faithfully trusting You!

In Jesus' Name, Amen

October 12

Do You See Those Who Need Your Help?

The Lord Jesus wants us to see with *His* eyes. There are people around us who need our help. Have you seen those who need you to touch them with kindness? The love you give will return to you as a blessing from God above. The peace you give will enter your heart when you serve from your heart. The joy you spread will double and multiply. The hope you bring will strengthen the weak and encourage you. It is more blessed to give than to receive! *"In all things I have shown you that by working hard in this way we must help the weak and remember the words of the Lord Jesus, how he himself said, 'It is more blessed to give than to receive,'"* Acts 20:35.

Dear Lord,

You want me to give love to those in need. Enlighten my eyes so I can see others through your eyes. Open the eyes of my heart to touch those who are struggling and need You. I will share the truth of the hope that is within me when I share Your love with others. It is more blessed to give than to receive!

In Jesus' Name, Amen

October 13

Are You Praying for God's Will to be Done?

We pray and then we patiently wait for answers. God hears our heart when we pray. He is always listening. Are you praying for God's will to be done? God speaks to you when you open your heart to Him, listen to Him, and obey Him. Ask faithfully for what is on your heart, seek the Lord by drawing closer to Him, and knock by continuing to pray for the door to be opened to you. As you wait on the Lord, your heart will rejoice because you feel His love overflowing in you! *"Let the will of the Lord be done,"* Acts 21:14.

Dear Lord,

I love praying to You. As I pray, I will wait upon You for Your will to be done. I am patient as You have always been patient with me. It took me a long time to be still enough to let go of self and see Your hand upon me. I am created new in You with the same Spirit living in me as the one who raised my Lord Jesus from death to life! I will hold on to You and keep faithfully praying for Your will to be done.

In Jesus' Name, Amen

October 14

Do You Need Courage?

We will face uncertainties in this life. Things will change and we will have to face challenges. With God, we can face anything because He never changes. He is the same yesterday, today, and forever. He is always constant and makes all things possible. In fact, He will give us courage and help us fight our battle! There is nothing He cannot do. He molded you in His image and created you to be in fellowship with Him. He wants a relationship with you because He loves you. Come closer to His love and be braver and bolder for the days ahead! He is with you and will strengthen you to be courageous! *"The Lord stood by him and said, "Take courage…"* Acts 23:11.

Dear Lord,

I know You will stand by me and strengthen me. I have courage to press on even in the face of adversity and challenge. Nothing can defeat me when I have You by my side. I am one step closer to my destiny when I let Your Spirit within me awaken me to new life with greater courage and hope for the days ahead!

In Jesus' Name, Amen

October 15

Are You Ready to Rise and Go?

You *can* rise and go. God has called you and will equip you for the challenges ahead. He needs you to get ready for what He needs you to do. As you listen, He will tell you. As you wait on Him, He will show you the path. As you trust Him, He will open your eyes to see and your heart to believe! It is time to rise, stand firm in your faith, and go with your confidence and security in the Lord! *"Rise and go..."*Acts 22:10.

Dear Lord,

When You call me, I will listen. When You need me, I will go. When I seek You, I will find the promises You have given me. You have promised me the gift of the Holy Spirit who will help, comfort, enrich, and strengthen me for what I need. You have sacrificed so that I can live in freedom and grace! It is by faith I have been saved! I will go by faith with Your blessings and power that are mine in Jesus Christ.

In Jesus' Name, Amen

October 16

Is Your Hope Set Upon God?

God is our living hope. When we trust Him, He will show us that hope can be found in His eternal promises. His promises remain true to eternity and are ours in Jesus Christ! Is your hope in the promises of God? His promises for you are precious and perfectly made with you in mind. Listen to Him calling you into a deeper relationship with Him and let His love cover every part of you with hope from heaven above! *"Having a hope in God…"* Acts 24:15.

Dear Lord,

My hope is found in You. I believe Your promises to me. I know You are for me and not against me. Everything You promise is true. You have brought hope to my life and love to my heart. I am stronger today because I have my hope set on You. I believe Your promises and know they are irrevocable. You have given me a living hope that lasts until eternity! I trust You and love You, my Lord of hope!

In Jesus' Name, Amen

October 17

Do You Believe You Can Hear Him?

God is speaking to you. Do you hear Him? As you pray and read His Word, you will hear what He is telling you. His whispers of love are gentle reminders of His presence. He hears your heart. Do you hear His? Listen with your heart and know He loves you. Rise and hear His voice calling you to arise and make a difference for His kingdom. No matter what is going on around you, God is able. *"You will hear him,"* Acts 25:22.

Dear Lord,

Thank You for speaking to me. I hear You calling me with gentle whispers of love. I know You love me and care about me. Thank You for opening my heart so I can hear You. It is well with my soul when I am close to You and feel you comforting me with Your love. I am thankful for the joy that is mine in Christ Jesus. As I pray, I will hear Your loving voice giving me direction. As I listen and obey, I will be showing my love for You! Speak Lord, for your servant is listening!

In Jesus' Name, Amen

October 18

Are You Worried?

In this world, we will have trouble, but Jesus promises to be our source of strength and power. Give Him your worries and let Him take them from you. He knows what you have been through in the past, what you are facing right now, and what you will face in the future! He is enough! Let go of what is troubling you and hold on tight to Jesus! Open your heart and let Him fill you with the Holy Spirit. His truth will guide and help you through anything you will face! Hear His voice telling you, *"Take heart, for there will be no loss of life among you, but only of the ship,"* Acts 27:22.

Dear Lord,

I have let You in my life, Lord, and my heart is Yours. I am taking heart because I know You love me eternally. There is hope in my heart because I trust You in all things and circumstances. There is joy and peace in me because I am free! It is well with my soul because You are my Lord and Savior forever! Praising You, Lord, the living hope of my heart, now and forevermore!

In Jesus' Name, Amen

October 19

Are Continuing to Speak so Others Can Hear the Joyful News?

There are people who need to hear the joyful news they are loved by God. He wants you to keep on speaking truth about your Savior and Redeemer to make a difference. He yearns for you to keep living out your faith so others may believe. It is time to speak and pray with boldness and without hindrance so others can listen, believe they are loved, and come to a living relationship with Jesus! *"They will listen,"* Acts 28:28.

Dear Lord,

I am counting my blessings today, beginning with my salvation. I have a relationship with You and have received the Holy Spirit into my life. Your gift has brought me new life. I have shed my old self and let You restore me into life as a new creation! I will keep sharing the hope of new life that is within me so others may believe and receive Your most gracious gifts of love, salvation, and the joy of the Holy Spirit! Behold God the Father, Jesus Christ, and the Holy Spirit!

In Jesus' Name, Amen

October 20

Have You Received Your Gift of Grace?

You are forgiven of your sins when you receive God's gift of grace through the blood of His Son, Jesus Christ. It is by His saving grace through faith in Jesus Christ that you are free. Grace is God's reward to you that came at Christ's expense. Have you opened your heart to believe and receive? God has much to give you when you trust Him and make Him Lord of your life. As you let His grace cover you, the peace of Christ will rule in your heart and you will receive His forgiveness for your sins. Grace always comes before peace. Open your heart and receive God's gift of grace! *"Receive forgiveness of sins..."* Acts 26:18.

Dear Lord,

I am free from my sins which have entangled me before I received Your gift of grace. You loved me so much You gave me Your only begotten Son as a sacrifice for my sins. The cross is proof of Your eternal love for me! I am drawing to Your throne of grace with confidence. I know Your peace will rule in my heart when I let Your grace in! I am forgiven in the name of Jesus Christ!

In Jesus' Name, Amen

October 21

Who Needs You?

God will be there for us wherever we go. He wants us to be strong and courageous so He can show us what He needs us to do. We do not need to be afraid to help when we have God on our side. Each of us has a wonderful opportunity to work for His Kingdom. We are blessed to join Him in the work He is already doing! There are exciting times ahead where we can make a difference in the lives of people. Seek God and be prepared for what He needs you to do. Be strong and courageous! Who can you encourage with God's love? *"Be strong and courageous. Do not be frightened, and do not be dismayed, for the LORD your God is with you wherever you go,"* Joshua 1:9.

Dear Lord,

I will be strong and courageous for the journey ahead. You have opportunities for me to serve You, Lord. I am listening to You. Even if it seems difficult, I know You will be my strength. I can hear Your voice encouraging me for what lies before me. I am humbled to work for You, Lord, for Your glory!

In Jesus' Name, Amen

October 22

Are You Walking by Faith?

God looks far and wide for people with great faith. Will He find such people on earth? Are we some of those people with great faith? As you live by faith believing God is able and not doubting what He promises, He is well pleased with you. God rewards those who remain faithful and live out what they believe. It is time to believe what God says is true even when you cannot see the details. Keep your faith and see the victory that is yours in Jesus Christ! "For we *walk by faith, not by sight,*" 2 Corinthians 5:7.

Dear Lord,

I know You want me to live by faith. You are pleased when I walk by faith and not by sight. I believe in Your promises and I will remain faithful to You, Lord! I see with eyes of faith because I trust in You. I am praying You will guide me into all truth and strengthen me to step out farther in faith. I know You are with me each step of the way when I walk by faith and not by sight!

In Jesus' Name, Amen

October 23

Is Your Faith Resting in the Power of God?

There is power and authority in the name of Jesus. He is mighty to forgive and save us. May our faith rest not in the wisdom of men, but in the power of God, given to us through Jesus Christ. As we enter a real relationship with Him, He will bless our lives and strengthen us. We are part of the family of God when we make Him the Lord of our lives. What blessings we will receive when we are sure of who our faith rests in! *"That your faith might not rest in the wisdom of men but in the power of God,"* 1 Corinthians 2:5

Dear Lord,

You have given me great hope as I trust You even more each day. I am walking by faith as I lean on You. Help me to continue trusting You in all areas of my life. I will stay focused on You and what You are calling me to do. You have a perfect plan for my life, and I am rejoicing knowing all is in Your hands! Give me courage and strength to press on!

In Jesus' Name, Amen

October 24

Are You Making the Most of
Your Days with the Lord?

Our days are numbered. We have a choice how we will live each day and who we will serve. When He is Lord of our life, He will put a heart of wisdom in us so we can make the most of each day. Listen, pray, trust, and obey God and He will show you the way. He will give you wisdom to make the best use of your time. Don't miss a single moment! It's time to rise and go! "S*o teach us to number our days that we might get a heart of wisdom,*" Psalm 90:12.

Dear Lord,

I do not want to miss anything You have for me! As I live with my eyes on You, You will show me what You need me to do. I am listening to Your promptings from the Holy Spirit and I am ready to go. I want to live in the moment. You have given me more opportunities to love. I am ready to live for You by making the most of these glorious days You have given me!

In Jesus' Name, Amen

October 25

Do You See the Wonders and Goodness of God All Around You?

God works wonders all around us with His mighty power and for His glory! Do you see the wonders of His love around you? He has shown His glory in the heavens above and on earth below. Look and see what God has done. There is evidence of His love and faithfulness. Let His Spirit touch your heart to believe. Open your heart to God's love and see His goodness and mercies that are new every morning! *"You are the God who works wonders; you have made known your might among the peoples,"* Psalm 77:14.

Dear Lord,

You have shown Your power and glory to me as I have made the decision to follow You. When I believed and made You Lord of my life, You put Your Spirit within me and strengthened me for the challenges ahead. I draw closer to You each day. I will keep my devotion to You as I look up and see Your wonders and I will stay focused on You as I walk by faith and not by sight!

In Jesus' Name, Amen

October 26

Are You Speaking Boldly About God's Truth?

God has good news for all who trust Him. He wants us to open our hearts to His truth found in the Word of God. There are still people who need to hear about Jesus to set them free. They are waiting for you to share your story for God's glory. Especially now, when conflict is all around you, God needs you to stand firm and share His love. There is a whole world out there that needs to know they are loved, and you have been given the courage through Jesus in you to speak boldly. Rise and go! *"We had boldness in our God to declare to you the gospel of God in the midst of much conflict,"* 1 Thessalonians 2:2.

Dear Lord,

Your love has encouraged me. Your truth has empowered me. Your Spirit has strengthened me. I will stand firm because I have Your Spirit and Your Word within me to give me courage to speak. Closed hearts are waiting to be opened by Your invitation of love. I will use the keys I have been given to bring others to know You!

In Jesus' Name, Amen

October 27

Are You a Conqueror?

We can conquer our fears as we let Christ live in and through us. He has promised to fight our battles when we trust Him. Are you struggling with what you cannot change? Has life become too burdensome? Have you given up because it is too hard for you? Nothing is too hard for God! Let go and let your heart be open to His help. Believe He has made you more than a conqueror because He loves you! *"We are more than conquerors through him who loved us,"* Romans 8:37.

Dear Lord,

Your love has touched the depths of my soul. I can be more than a conqueror as I trust You to fight for me. I will not listen to the doubting voices that try to confuse and defeat me. I will look to the hope I have found in You. I will trust You more and walk by faith. I am more than a conqueror because You have conquered all my sins at the cross and won the victory for me. I believe in You, Lord Jesus, with all my heart!

In Jesus' Name, Amen

October 28

Have You Been Set Free by Jesus?

Jesus Christ will set you free! Hear this truth and believe! Listen and wholeheartedly trust Your Savior to give You new life. The darkness disappears when you follow His light. Hope fills your heart and warms your soul when you make Him Lord of your life. As you obey, you will find freedom from sin that has separated you from God. There is no other way to be free than through the Son of God. He gifted you grace so you can walk away from sin and come closer to His love. Has the Son set you free? *"For freedom Christ has set us free..."* Galatians 5:1.

Dear Lord,

I am free, indeed, because of You! I am whole because You have saved me. I have new life because You put Your Spirit within me. I am praising You today for the eternal love You give me! I will walk in the light of Your hope and believe Your promises for me. No one can convince me otherwise or separate me from Your love! In You, Jesus Christ, I am free, indeed!

In Jesus' Name, Amen

October 29

Are You Letting the Lord Open Your Heart?

Your heart can be opened by the Lord so you can hear what He wants to share with you. Are you letting the Lord open your heart? When you do, He will show you wonderful things that will bless you richly. He will help you see what He needs you to see. He will open the eyes of your heart as you draw closer to His presence. He will show you the way to go as the Holy Spirit guides you into all truth. He wants to speak truth to you. Surrender to Him and the Holy Spirit will magnify your soul! *"The Lord opened her heart to pay attention..."* Acts 16:14.

Dear Lord,

You have opened my heart so I can pay close attention to You. I am listening and I am praying for more revelation. My heart is open to what You want to show me. You will show me Your glory and strengthen me more each day with the power of the Holy Spirit. I will continue paying close attention. Speak Lord, for Your servant is listening with her heart!

In Jesus' Name, Amen

October 30

Are You Living and Moving
with the Holy Spirit Inside You?

You can live and move and be empowered by the Holy Spirit inside you when you follow Christ. He wants to be present *in* you. The God of hope will fill you with joy and peace when you believe and live empowered by the Holy Spirit. Are you struggling to believe you can live and move and have your being in Him? Instead of doubting, try trusting Christ for everything you need. To live is Christ with His glorious riches and spiritual blessings, and to die is gain with the promise of eternal life! *"In him we live and move and have our being..."* Acts 17:28.

Dear Lord,

Oh, how I love and trust You for all my needs. There is nothing You cannot do. With You, all things are possible! I will trust You in everything. I know You placed Your Spirit in me for Your glory. As I surrender all, You will give me an empowered life connected to the Holy Spirit. I am blessed beyond measure with spiritual blessings in Christ, redemption in Christ, and an inheritance in Christ!

In Jesus' Name, Amen

October 31

Are You Afraid to Speak From Your Heart?

The Lord wants you to continue speaking from your heart. He will be with you always, so say what you need to say and honor Him. If you keep silent, people will not know the hope that is theirs in Jesus Christ. If you do not reach out in love, many will not know they are loved. Be a light of love by sharing the hope that is within you. People are counting on your love and encouragement. Keep believing and shining the light of the love that is within you! *"Do not be afraid, but go on speaking and do not be silent,"* Acts 18:9.

Dear Lord,

Your Word is clear to me and I am enriched in every way by the direction and hope You give me. You need me to share love through words of hope and acts of service. You loved me first. Your cross is the proof love made the first move. You are always with me when I share hope through words and deeds empowered by the Holy Spirit!

In Jesus' Name, Amen

Monthly Reflections

As you pray and lean on the Lord's promises, write what the Lord has revealed to you for this month.

Give thanks
IN ALL
CIRCUMSTANCES;
FOR THIS IS
the will of God
in Christ Jesus
for you.
1 THESSALONIANS 5:18

November 1

Do You Hear the Voice
of the Good Shepherd?

Jesus is calling you! Do you hear His voice? Will you follow Him? He has tried to get your full attention for some time now. He needs you to come to Him just as you are. Leave your fears and trust the one who will never leave or forsake you. Believe He has your best interests at heart and that He has wonderful plans with you in mind. You do not need to be afraid to take the next step closer to your Good Shepherd. You are one of His sheep, so listen and trust Him to lead you! *"My sheep hear my voice, and I know them, and they follow me,"* John 10:27.

Dear Lord,

I will stay close to You and follow Your voice. There are so many other voices that try to pull me away from the truth. I will not listen to them, but will listen to You, Jesus, because you are wonderful to me! My heart rejoices when I hear You calling me! Thank You for teaching me and reaching me with Your love and grace. You are my Good Shepherd!

In Jesus' Name, Amen

November 2

Do You Feel Defeated?

The Lord wants to defend you, so come out of your defeat. When you need help, He will be a shield of strength and protection for you and the lifter of your head. He lifts you up to come closer to His love. Talk to Him about what is burdening you. Let Him fight this battle you are facing! Have you been letting your problems overcome you instead of clinging to God's promises? Trust God and see that He is there for you. There is hope in all the promises of God. Write them on your heart and believe! *"I cried aloud to the LORD, and he answered me from his holy hill,"* Psalm 3:4.

Dear Lord,

Thank You for lifting me up with Your promises that give me hope! Your shield about me keeps me from being defeated, depressed, and discouraged. I know, when I call to You, You will help me fight this battle raging around me. I do not have to let the problems consume me because there is always hope when I cling tighter to You! Your way leads to righteousness and Your path is full of promise!

In Jesus' Name, Amen

November 3

Are You Having Trouble Sleeping?

God wants us to rest in His peace so we can sleep. Meditate on God's promises and rest in His presence. He is there to comfort us when we need comfort and rest. He is near when we call upon Him for help. Pray for God to help you find rest. *Blessed are the poor in spirit, for theirs is the kingdom of heaven. Blessed are those who mourn, for they shall be comforted,"* Matthew 5:3-4. You are blessed by God just when you need Him! He is there for you whenever you need Him, day or night. Call upon Him and He will come to help you lie down and sleep in His peace.

Dear Lord,

When I am restless, I know that I need to be still and draw closer to You in prayer. It is so good to know Your peace that warms every part of me like a blanket of love. I am thankful Your love covers me from head to toe and inside and out. I can lie down and sleep in peace when I cling tighter to You, Lord. I am blessed when I am in Your presence!

In Jesus' Name, Amen

November 4

Do You Need a Helper?

Jesus has given you another Helper that the world cannot receive because they do not believe. But you believe and have this gift from Jesus inside you. Do you need help? Be still and listen to the sound of the still, small voice inside of you. The Holy Spirit is calling you to hold on to the hope that is within you and press on to peace that comes from His presence. Receive your gift of the Holy Spirit! He is your Helper.

Dear Lord,

When I need direction and truth, You show me the light. When I need strength, You give me Your power. When this new life flows through me, every part of me tingles, in my body, soul, and spirit. I am alive as You promise in John 14:16, "*And I will ask the Father, and he will give you another Helper, to be with you forever.*"

In Jesus' Name, Amen

November 5

Are You Abiding in the Love of Jesus?

Have you felt the love of Jesus in your life? Jesus loves you and wants you to abide in Him by giving Him your heart. He has so much to show you when you make time for Him. You will not know Jesus unless you abide in His love. Do you hear the heartbeat of the Holy Spirit inside you? You *will* if you abide in the love of Jesus and let His presence empower you!

Dear Lord,

You have promised to love me as I abide in Your love. I feel Your presence in my life as I abide in you. You have calmed my spirit and warmed my heart with Your love. I feel Your heartbeat of love throughout my heart, body, and soul. Your promise in John 15:9 comforts me as I abide in You. *"As the Father has loved me, so have I loved you. Abide in my love."*

In Jesus' Name, Amen

November 6

Have You Asked in the Name of Jesus?

Jesus brings us joy. When we ask Him for what is on our hearts, He hears us. You *have* not because you *ask* not. Seek Him and ask for what you need in the name of Jesus. The prayers not prayed cannot be answered. There are unspoken prayers Jesus is waiting to answer for you. As you speak, He will hear you. As you pray, He will answer, and your joy will be full!

Dear Lord,

Your word says in John 16:24, *"Until now you have asked nothing in my name. Ask, and you will receive, that your joy may be full."* I will keep asking for what I need so You will answer. I desire Your joy that comes to me when I continue praying believing nothing is impossible with you!

In Jesus' Name, Amen

November 7

Have You Been Praying
in the Spirit with Power?

The prayers of a righteous person are working because they have great power. When you pray in the Spirit of God, God will move to answer for *His* glory. He hears your prayers and will answer you! Are you praying with all the power inside you? God of all power knows what you need, and He delights to answer you. Keep in step with the Spirit inside you and pray from your heart with all gladness and joy. Believe there are answers that are just a prayer away!

Dear Lord,

When I need You, I can reach out and pray. When my heart is heavy, You will hear my cries for help. When I sing Your praises, You are well pleased because You love a grateful heart. My heart knows You will be faithful to me every moment as I patiently wait upon You. Your patience and goodness are a breath of fresh air to my soul and my spirit! *"The prayer of a righteous person has great power as it is working,"* James 5:16.

In Jesus' Name, Amen

November 8

Do You Believe that with
God All Things Are Possible?

When we take God with us in all circumstances, He will make all things possible. It is possible for God to do what seems impossible. Have you taken God with you in the situations you are facing? Are you joyfully asking for His guidance even in impossible situations? He is waiting for you to ask Him. He yearns to help you with all that you face. Keep believing and keep asking for God to show up for you! He will never fail you but will show you great and mighty things that can happen when you take Him with you in all that you do! *"For nothing will be impossible with God,"* Luke 1:37.

Dear Lord,

I do believe all things are possible with You! I am taking You with me because I need You, Lord. I know You can help me and I believe I will see greater things when I am present in Your presence. My heart is wide open to believe in the impossible!

In Jesus' Name, Amen

November 9

Have You Found Your Life in Jesus?

You will find life when you lose it for the sake of Christ. He desires that you walk with Him in the Spirit and not the flesh. He wants you to lose your life of flesh for His sake. What does this mean for you? Are you living your life where Jesus is your Lord? When He is Lord of your life, there will be peace and joy and a rush of the Holy Spirit in your inner being. A fresh wind of the Spirit will invade your soul to refresh and revive you. Forsaking all, but pursuing a simple pursuit of Jesus, will give you the life you are seeking. *"Whoever finds his life will lose it, and whoever loses his life for my sake will find it,"* Matthew 10:39.

Dear Lord,

I will pursue You to find life. In this world, there are temptations and desires that take me away from you. I will seek more of You and not the ways of the world. You are there in the stillness of my soul and in the chaos around me. No one can take me away from You!

In Jesus' Name, Amen

November 10

Are You Answering Others Softly?

We have the choice about how we will answer others. When we answer softly, people listen and respond with gladness. But when we answer with harsh words, anger stirs up. Jesus wants us to answer kindly with words of love. This will bring peace to every situation. How will you answer when you are challenged? This is a question we will all have to answer as we live in a world of good and evil. Respond the way Jesus wants and You will be rewarded. *"Let your speech always be gracious, seasoned with salt, so that you may know how you ought to answer each person,"* Colossians 4:6.

Dear Lord,

I know that I will be challenged in this world. The attacks will come, but I know You will help me in my response. You were attacked and responded with love and forgiveness. You carried all my sins as people crucified You. But death did not defeat You! Because I have received Your amazing grace, I will respond with a soft heart and season my words with grace.

In Jesus' Name, Amen

November 11

Did You Know Jesus Prays for You?

Jesus Christ prays for you. He wants you to know He lifts you up to His Father. He intercedes for you as He brings your prayers to the throne of God. Kneel before Jesus and lift your prayers to Him. As you bow before the King, be confident and secure knowing He prays mightily for you as He prays to the Father. In John 17:9 he says, *"I am not praying for the world but for those whom you have given me, for they are yours."*

Dear Lord,

Thank You for praying for me! I know You love me when you hear my prayers and intercede for me. My heart is overwhelmed with joy knowing You pray for me as I sit at Your feet and worship You. My soul is rejuvenated. A fresh fire ignites inside me. The Holy Spirit has awakened and revived me as I listen to Your whispers of love!

In Jesus' Name, Amen

November 12

Are You Sharing the Hope Within You?

The gospel of God brings life and power to us and there is salvation for everyone who believes. For when we receive and live out the message from within the gospel, we will know the power that is ours in Christ! God wants to set us free as we listen to truth found in His Word. He yearns for us to believe. He wants us to spread the message of hope far and wide. Are you sharing the good news of the gospel? *"For I am not ashamed of the gospel, for it is the power of God for salvation to everyone who believes, to the Jew first and also to the Greek,"* Romans 1:16.

Dear Lord,

I have hope in Your gospel of life! There is power in it for me as I believe. My salvation is secure in You, Lord, as I receive grace upon grace. I am living out my faith, without fear, as I live for You each moment. I will share my hope I have found in You!

In Jesus' Name, Amen

November 13

Do Know God has Called You to Live a Life of Godliness?

God wants us to trust Him to show us the way to a life of godliness. He knows we will live in His power when we completely trust Him. He gives us knowledge and power to live in His glory. Are you taking God with you in all areas of your life? What about living in His presence? It is a simple trust that God wants from you. Trust Him with all your heart and lean not on your own understanding so He can make your path straight! Then You will know this power that only God can give you! *"His divine power has granted to us all things that pertain to life and godliness, through the knowledge of him who called us to his own glory and excellence,"* 2 Peter 1:3.

Dear Lord

I will trust You with all my heart and not lean on my own understanding. With You, there is power and knowledge. I can live a life of godliness when I let you rule inside me. I see that Your glory and excellence are mine when I live close to You!

In Jesus' Name, Amen

November 14

Are You Seeking the Lord?

The Lord wants you to seek Him and live. He has set you apart as His child whom He has chosen. When you let Him lead you, He will set your feet on solid ground. There are many ways for you to go, but only *one* way that will lead to life—God's way. Let the Lord's love flood your heart so you will know Him intimately. Are you rooted and firmly established in Him? Ask yourself this question and answer it with a resounding yes! *"Seek the Lord and live…"* Amos 5:6.

Dear Lord,

I am set free in You when my feet are solidly planted in the soil of Your Word. I have found life and my soul is on fire with Your Spirit. I will seek You all the days of my life and smell the sweet aroma of Your presence as I live each day in Your never-ending love. My heart is set on You, my Lord, as I seek to live with You eternally!

In Jesus' Name, Amen

November 15

Whom Do You Follow?

The Lord is your Shepherd. Are you following Him? He will give you everything you need when you keep Him first in your life. Does the Lord have first place in your heart? When He reigns in you, all your other wants seem to disappear. Keep seeking Your Lord and trust Him for all you need. Follow Him, and He will meet the deepest needs of your heart and soul! *"The LORD is my shepherd; I shall not want. He makes me lie down in green pastures. He leads me beside still waters." Psalm 23:1-2.*

Dear Lord,

Because You are my Shepherd, I have everything I need in You. It is my desire to follow You all the days of my life. I know You will lead me where I need to go. As I pray to You, I feel Your power comforting me. As I listen and obey You, I feel Your favor overwhelming me. As I sit still in Your presence, I feel Your love overpowering me!

In Jesus' Name, Amen

November 16

Is the Lord Your Strength?

God will strengthen you for everything that lies ahead. He knows what you need and when you need to be infused with strength for challenges. Listen to His direction and let Him make you stronger. When you are weak, He is strong. Are you loving the Lord with all your heart? Are you asking Him to help you? He loves you so much and will be a very present help to you! *"I love you, O LORD, my strength,"* Psalm 18:1.

Dear Lord,

Thank You, Lord, for your help and comfort. When I am weak, I know you will be my strength. I need not fear anything that tries to weaken me or anyone who comes against me. Your love has brought hope to my life in many amazing ways even in my weakest moments. I am grateful to You, my Lord, my strength!

In Jesus' Name, Amen

November 17

Do You Have Fullness of Joy?

In the presence of God, there is fullness of joy and at His right hand are pleasures forevermore! Are you looking for utmost joy in your life? Do you want to have joy in all your circumstances? It is only possible to have this kind of joy when you have a close relationship with Jesus. He will give you joy no matter what you are facing. His joy comes at *all* times and in *all* situations where His presence reigns! "*You make known to me the path of life; in your presence there is fullness of joy; at your right hand are pleasures forevermore,*" Psalm 16:11.

Dear Lord,

I know fullness of joy reigns when You are present in my life. I will keep close to You, my Lord, in all circumstances. You are the treasure I seek and my heart's desire. I love being close to You, my Lord. Where my treasure is, there my heart is also, and that place is with You!

In Jesus' Name, Amen

November 18

Do You Need Assurance?

God will grant your heart's desires when you keep seeking His will and desires for you. He wants what is best for you. That should encourage you amongst all the uncertainty. Need some assurance about your plans? God will fulfill His plans for your life when you give Him your whole heart and seek His way. He is your way-maker. He will always make a way for you! *"May he grant you your heart's desire and fulfill all your plans,"* Psalm 20:4.

Dear Lord,

Thank You for making a way for me when there seems to be no way. I know You will fulfill my heart's desire when I trust You and Your will for my life. When I need help, all I need to do is call upon You. You are patiently waiting. I am trusting Your timing to fulfill what You place on my heart. Show me the way and I will follow!

In Jesus' Name, Amen

November 19

Do You Know You Are a Child of God?

God our Father has given you His Spirit because you are His child. He loves you dearly. He bears witness with your Spirit so you can know His will for you. He wants you to know that He desires the best for you. He is God Almighty who knows everything about you. As you live for Him, He will show His limitless love for you. The proof of His love is found at the cross. Because of His sacrifice, you can live! Keep listening to His Spirit and believe you are loved! *"The Spirit himself bears witness with our spirit that we are children of God,"* Romans 8:16.

Dear Lord,

I know I am loved by You! Thank You for giving me Your Holy Spirit so I can know Your eternal love. I believe I am Your heir with an eternal inheritance that cannot be taken away from me! This truth is beautiful music to my ears! I am a child of grace and love filled with the power of the Holy Spirit!

In Jesus' Name, Amen

November 20

Do You Hear?

God is speaking to you. Do you hear Him? Listen to His Word and let it change Your mind and Your heart. God has spoken life to You, dear child. He is ready for you to listen so He can pour His life-giving Spirit into you. There are many things that He wants to say to you. Your faith will come when you hear Him. Listen and believe what God is telling you and see your faith grow! "S*o faith comes from hearing, and hearing through the word of Christ*," Romans 10:17.

Dear Lord,

I know You have called me to continue walking faithfully in Your truth. You have asked me to listen wisely and carefully to You. There are new wonders you want to show me, but I need to listen and hear You through the Word of life found in the Bible. I need to read it prayerfully and with patience. I will find purpose as I live passionately for You. Your Word has come to life in me! Hallelujah!

In Jesus' Name, Amen

November 21

Are You Considering Others Before Yourself?

Jesus, as an example for us to follow, was humble and kind to everyone. He loved others more than He loved himself. He sacrificed His life for our freedom and poured His mercy and grace over us. Are you forgiving and showing grace to others? Are you seeking out the lost, lonely, and hopeless? Are you reaching out to share the love of Jesus? Love as Christ has loved you—with a humble heart doing everything out of love and respect. When you do others may find Christ! *"Do nothing from selfish ambition or conceit, but in humility count others more significant than yourselves,"* Philippians 2:3.

Dear Lord,

Help me continue the race of life. With my eyes fixed on You, I will see others as more important than myself. Glory to You, God, for shining Your light in me and giving me unshakable hope each day. I will press on towards the goal, my prize, Christ Jesus!

In Jesus' Name, Amen

November 22

Are You Building Yourself
Up Through Prayer?

We must persevere in our faith as we keep ourselves in the love of God with the Holy Spirit inside us. Even when we see division and strife, we keep praying in the Holy Spirit for unity and peace. It is true that we live in a world of chaos where people are living selfishly. The Lord hurts when He sees His people turning away from Him to follow their own desires. Build up your faith by spending time with the Lord in prayer and join with others who are praying in the Holy Spirit so you can be encouraged in your own race. *"But you, beloved, building yourselves up in your most holy faith and praying in the Holy Spirit,"* Jude 20.

Dear Lord,

Thank You for giving me mercy and grace even when I have turned away from You. I am praying with the power of the Holy Spirit You placed inside me. I will build my faith by spending time with You in prayer and reading Your Word.

In Jesus' Name, Amen

November 23

Are You Seeking God in His Word?

Receive the implanted word of the Lord with humility and meekness as you search for answers or seek direction in your life. The treasures in God's Word will save your soul. The truth found within the Bible is like a seed that continually grows inside of you. It changes you from the inside out. Your heart, mind, and soul will be transformed when you seek the truth and obey it. Love the Lord, obey His commands, and remain in Him as you seek His wise counsel daily. When you are one with the Lord, He will change your life! *"Therefore put away all filthiness and rampant wickedness and receive with meekness the implanted word, which is able to save your souls,"* James 1:21.

Dear Lord,

I will apply Your truth to my life by doing what You say. I will turn to You with all meekness and receive new life in You. I know You are giving me comfort, peace, and joy when I let You counsel and speak to me through the pages of the Holy Bible. Only You can transform me from the inside out!

In Jesus' Name, Amen

November 24

Are You Trusting the Lord
with All Your Heart?

Trust in the Lord with *all* your heart, always placing Him in the forefront of your life. Pour out your heart before Him. God is your refuge and strength, and He is a very present help in trouble. He is right beside you ready to catch you when you fall and hold you up when you are weak. He will be your rock in the times of difficulty and times of peace. Trust Him to lead you. He makes all things possible to those who trust Him with all their hearts. Forever His Word is fixed in the heavens! *"Trust in him at all times, O people; pour out your heart before him; God is a refuge for us,"* Psalm 62:8.

Dear Lord,

If I ask in the name of Jesus and in Your will, Lord, I will receive. You love to give to Your children. I will be bold in my prayers in the name of Jesus. You are waiting to give me all my heart desires as I delight in You, Lord. I seek Your will for my life.

In Jesus' Name, Amen

November 25

Do You Know God Hems You In?

The Lord knows you from the inside out. He knows your thoughts and your desires. He is with you when you lay down and when you rise. He hems you in, behind and before Him, with His hand covering you. He is your safe place. Your refuge. Remain in Him and be still and know that He is God. His hand will lead you through the darkest times as He holds you firmly. *"You hem me in, behind and before, and lay your hand upon me,"* Psalm 139:5.

Dear Lord,

I know I am precious to You, the one who formed me in my mother's womb. I am fearfully and wonderfully made in the image of You, Lord. You loved me even before I was born. I am breathing in Your Spirit and feel Your peace covering me like a warm, soft blanket. Your touch has opened my heart and soul to a new hunger for You and my cup is overflowing with the greatest joy. I have put my trust in You! I have tasted Your living water and I will never be thirsty again!

In Jesus' Name, Amen

November 26

Are You Rejoicing?

Rejoice in the Lord always! The Lord wants you to come to Him with all your requests and praise Him for His blessings. His light shines through you and in you as a child of God. Do not be anxious about anything but pray about everything with thanksgiving. He will supply every need of yours according to His will for you in Christ Jesus. Give Him glory and praise for His answers to your prayers. In times of need, keep praying, rejoicing, and trusting. Trust that His plan for you is good and that He knows what is best for you! *"Rejoice in the Lord always; again I will say, rejoice*!" Philippians 4:4.

Dear Lord,

Your peace has settled in my heart the more I trust You. I am joyful in hope, patient in affliction, and persistent in prayer, giving thanks to You, God, in all my circumstances. I will rise above my circumstances and shine Your light for all the world to see. Again and again I will rejoice, for You, Lord, are good all the time!

In Jesus' Name, Amen

November 27

Is the Word of God Dwelling Inside You?

Let the word of God dwell in you richly as you worship Him with a thankful heart. As you do, you will sing psalms of praise and hymns with joy. God is alive in your heart when you let His Word rule in your mind. Is the Word of God dwelling richly in you? Let the peace of Christ rule in your heart and put on His love which binds everything together in perfect harmony. Proclaim the mystery of Christ found in the gospel and walk with Him in confidence knowing He is all you need. Set your mind on the things above, starting with the Word of God. *"Let the word of God dwell in you richly, teaching and admonishing one another in all wisdom, singing psalms and hymns and spiritual songs, with thankfulness in your hearts to God,"* Colossians 3:16.

Dear Lord,

I will glorify You in all I do and let the power of the Holy Spirit work in my life by guiding me into all truth. As I seek Your kingdom and all Your righteousness, all good things will be added to me in Your mighty and powerful name. You will reign in me when I find my home in You, O Lord!

In Jesus' Name, Amen

November 28

Where Does Your Faith Rest?

Are you putting your faith in the power of God? God will give you power from the Holy Spirit who sustains you and carries you throughout your life. When you are weak, He will be your strength. When you are afraid, He will fight for you. Take His hand and go with Him to places where no eye has seen, no ear has heard, and no heart has imagined. He has searched you and knows every part of you. He sees your brokenness and knows your fears. Take these things captive and lay them before the Lord. *"What no eye has seen, nor ear heard, nor the heart of man imagined, what God has prepared for those who love him—"* 1 Corinthians 2:9.

Dear Lord,

I feel Your nearness and I am resting in Your presence. I will boast in You, Lord, and see Your love flow through me to others around me as I proclaim Your glory. You are the source of my faith. I will proclaim Your excellence and see Your power work in all things! Your power brings peace on earth and good will to all who choose to see You!

In Jesus' Name, Amen

November 29

Do You Really Believe?

Everyone who believes in Jesus Christ will have eternal life. Jesus invites you to believe the message—that He died for your salvation and eternal inheritance. When you accept His love and grace, He lives inside you. As you surrender all to Jesus, He will give you another Helper, the Holy Spirit, who dwells within you and gives you the power of hope, love, joy and peace. Have you surrendered all to Jesus? He will deliver you and set you apart as you soar high with His mighty power inside of you. Your heavenly reward is everlasting! *"That whoever believes in Him may have eternal life,"* John 3:15.

Dear Lord,

I have Your joy. It rings true for me because I have believed. I am encouraged by Your presence and seek Your promises for my life. I am hopeful in what You have promised me. You strengthen my soul each day. You magnify me!

In Jesus' Name, Amen

November 30

Are You Continuing the Work God Has for You?

For it is God who works in you both to will and to work for His good pleasure. As you obey and trust Him, Your faith in action will please the Lord. Allow the Spirit inside you to bring light to the dark places of the world. As you work, stand firm with other believers in one spirit with one mind striving side by side for the faith of the gospel. The Lord is raising up an army of warriors to fight His good fight of faith to the end. *"For it is God who works in you, both to will and to work for his good pleasure,"* Philippians 2:13.

Dear Lord,

Thank You for always being by my side. I have the armor I need for victory because I know You will fight my battles. You are the one who began a good work in me and the one who will bring it to completion at the day of Jesus Christ. I will work heartily for Christ and not for men. You long to see me working for Your good pleasure. My reward is found in Christ alone!

In Jesus' Name, Amen

Monthly Reflections

As you pray and lean on the Lord's promises, write what the Lord has revealed to you for this month.

GLORY TO GOD
IN THE HIGHEST,
and on earth
PEACE
among those with whom
he is pleased.

December 1

Do You Believe Even When You Do Not See?

Faith is born in the hearts of those that can look beyond their circumstances and believe without seeing. Faith grows as we trust in the Lord, knowing He will do what He has promised to do. Faith is the assurance of things hoped for and conviction of things not seen. Let us walk obediently by faith and not by sight. We must fix our eyes on Jesus, the author and perfecter of our faith. For the joy that was set before Him, He endured the cross and is seated at the right hand of the throne of God. Through the cross, we can have a new covenant relationship with the Father. *"Blessed are those who have not seen and yet have believed,"* John 20:29.

Dear Lord

I am pursuing Your steadfast love and immovable faith knowing You, Lord, are always faithful to me. I believe even though I do not see all the details. I love You with eyes of faith as I see You working in me.

In Jesus' Name, Amen

December 2

Are You Standing on the Rock?

You are stronger because of your trials and hardships. Your faith grows deeper each day when your heart is connected to Christ. You can stand on your rock, your Lord Jesus Christ, and put your faith in the only one who will save you. Are you standing on the rock? Look upon your Lord in His sanctuary and behold His power and glory. Magnify the Lord and exalt the name that is higher than any other name. His steadfast love extends to the heavens and His faithfulness to the clouds. Take refuge in the Lord, your firm foundation. All other ground is unstable and changing. *"He only is my rock and my salvation, my fortress; I shall not be shaken,"* Psalm 62:6.

Dear Lord,

I know You never change. As I commit my way to You and trust You, I know You will act. My steps are established in You. I delight in You and stand on You, my rock. My hope is in You, Lord, and I will not be shaken!

In Jesus' Name, Amen

December 3

Are You Drawing Close to God?

God hears you calling in the night. He will answer you. Keep praying and asking, because if you do not ask, you will not receive. He delights in your prayers and your praises and answers your pleas for healing. As you purify and submit your heart to the Lord by confessing your sins, you will be healed. The prayers of a righteous person have great power and are working. Lean on the power of Christ inside you and stand on His promises! When you submit to the Lord, deeply believe and you will see the mighty hand of God exalting you at the proper time. Humble yourself before the Lord and He will exalt you! *"Draw near to God and he will draw near to you..."* James 4:8.

Dear Lord,

I know that You can do far more than I can ask or think according to the power at work within me. As I continue loving others and serving the Lord with eagerness and gladness, I will experience a life of full faith and joy. The joy of the Lord is my strength!

In Jesus' Name, Amen

December 4

Are You Overcoming Evil With Good?

God rejoices when you are at peace with your brothers and sisters. He wants you to hold fast to what is good and continue walking in righteousness. You were made to be a peacemaker. The Lord will repay the unrighteous as He desires. Let Him be the judge and you do what is good. By your love, others will know your Lord because they see Jesus in you. Are you loving your enemies and forgiving the ones who have hurt you? Jesus was mocked, persecuted, beaten, and put to death, and yet, He showed them mercy and grace. He loved the very ones who hated Him. He forgave the ones who betrayed Him. He prayed to the Father to forgive them. Will you do the same? *"Do not be overcome by evil, but overcome evil with good,"* Romans 12:21.

Dear Lord,

I will live peacefully by forgiving those who have hurt me. I will be set free from my anger, bitterness, and hatred as I forgive. I am free because the Holy Spirit has rested upon me and peace has flooded my soul!

In Jesus' Name, Amen

December 5

What is on Your Mind?

We have a choice about where we set our mind. We can choose to focus on the world and its problems, or we can set our minds on the Lord. He wants to transform our minds. God wants to be our very present help. He will help us look at situations differently, so we see how big He is and not how big our problems are. It is in the darkest times where God shines in us the brightest! Let Him shine on you! *"Do not be conformed to this world, but be transformed by the renewal of your mind..."* Romans 12:2.

Dear Lord,

Only You can transform me, Lord. My mind will be renewed when I focus on You and what You can do *in* and *through* me. I am letting go of my problems that are trying to control my mind and stepping into life and peace in Your presence. Each day will be brighter as I stay close at heart to You!

In Jesus' Name, Amen

December 6

Are You Encouraging
the Next Generation?

Are you a part of the generation of believers that are leading the next generation? The Lord wants us to do our part to share the truth of His Word and the power of the Holy Spirit. As we share the knowledge of how great our God is, they will find strength in hopeless situations. God will reveal His glory through His mighty acts! We are to be doers of the word by leading, teaching, sharing, giving, and loving the next generation! *"One generation shall commend your works to another, and shall declare your mighty acts,"* Psalm 145:4.

Dear Lord,

I am striving to accomplish the plans you have laid for me, and I am striving to trust You without seeing all the details. I know You want me to serve You with my whole heart. As I work, I am planting seeds in the hearts of future leaders for Christ. I will not grow weary of doing good, for at the proper time, I know I shall see the harvest. I will stay the course and finish the great task for Your glory!

In Jesus' Name, Amen

December 7

Do You Fear the Lord?

When you hear the phrase, *the fear of the Lord,* what do you think about? Does your fear of the Lord your God make you look to Him for power, wisdom, and knowledge? His power will be your strength and His wisdom will fill you with knowledge. To fear Him is to trust in the Lord with all your heart. You cannot trust Him if you do not know Him. Get to know the Lord better each day by spending time with Him by prayer and reading His Word. You will know Him when you seek Him. Spend your days wisely by seeking the Lord at every turn and feel His love for you. *"The fear of the LORD is the beginning of knowledge; fools despise wisdom and instruction,"* Proverbs 1:7.

Dear Lord,

I know You will show me the way to live and will direct my path if I spend time listening to You. I will find all I need when I come to You with my heart wide open. I am living with Your grace and Your hope when I live connected to Your Word and Your Spirit. With You, I am fulfilled all the days of my life!

In Jesus' Name, Amen

December 8

Who is Jesus to You?

Jesus saves and He brings life. He is patiently waiting for you to make your home in Him. Is Jesus your peace? He knows in this world you will face trouble, but with Him, You can have peace. Are you breathing in the joy of the Holy Spirit? Jesus brings the gift of joy through the Holy Spirit that spills over to all areas of your life. Be still and know that He is God and see His glory shine upon you! Who is He to you? He is asking you, *"But who do you say that I am?"* Mark 8:29.

Dear Lord,

I am sitting still in this moment to reflect on Your glory and power in my life. I know You want me to be still and know You are God. I will keep striving to know You and spend time with You day after day. Each moment deepens my faith on this journey. There is peace and joy in the journey as I walk with You, my Lord and Savior!

In Jesus' Name, Amen

December 9

Are You Afraid to Speak Up?

Do not be afraid when the Lord commands you to speak. He will put His words in your mouth. Trust Him. The words He gives you to speak will declare His witness in a mighty way. The Lord knows what is on your mind. As you take every thought captive and evaluate them in light of His Word, He will renew your mind, restore your soul, and revive your heart. You have a new identity in Christ. As you grow in Christ, you will be made new as your old self will pass away and your new self will be born again! Cling to Christ and keep speaking from your heart! *"Behold, I have put my words in your mouth,"* Jeremiah 1:9.

Dear Lord,

I know I will grow good fruit when I am firmly planted in You. This sweet fruit will satisfy my every desire and will be enough for me to share with others. As I share, new seeds will produce more good fruit for You. This fruit of the Spirit is never out of season. As I speak, I will spread seeds of hope where miracles will bloom in due time!

In Jesus' Name, Amen

December 10

Are You Walking in Love?

Are you reaching out to others out of kindness that flows from a loving heart? Are you in need of genuine love from a friend who cares? Have you felt unloved at times? You are not alone when you have the love of Jesus. He loves you unconditionally. He notices you and loves you with His steadfast love. He is encouraging you to share His love with others. He never stops loving you! The love of Jesus is the key that opens the heart all the time! *"And walk in love, as Christ loved us and gave himself up for us, a fragrant offering and sacrifice to God,"* Ephesians 5:2.

Dear Lord,

Help me to stop *talking* about love and start *walking* in love like You desire. I will begin by listening to Your voice directing me as You say, "Follow my lead in deeds of love." I commit to love. Your love is the key that will open hearts to You!

In Jesus' Name, Amen

December 11

Are You Communicating with God?

Prayer is the way to communicate with God. As you lift each prayer to your Father in the name of Jesus, He bends down to listen to you right then. When you pray from your heart, you open the door to a deeper relationship with Him. He longs to give you what you need, but have you asked Him? If the answer is no, there is a better plan that only the Lord knows. If the answer is not now, the Lord wants you to keep praying to grow your faith while you wait. And if the answer is yes, He wants you to be thankful and give glory to your Father in Heaven so that others may believe. Keep praying, because all your prayers are beautiful to Him!

Dear Lord,

When I do not know what to pray, I know you will give me the words to say. Thank you for interceding for me. I humble myself before You. *"For we do not know what to pray for as we ought, but the Spirit himself intercedes for us with groanings too deep for words,"* Romans 8:26.

In Jesus' Name, Amen

December 12

Do You Feel the Touch of the Spirit?

We all have a Helper to guide, direct, and lead us in our decisions and give us direction for our lives. When we invite Jesus to live in our hearts, we have the presence of the gentle whisper of the Holy Spirit, our Helper. He gently guides us with His powerful love when we choose to live in the Spirit. As we surrender our hearts to His love, we can know how He wants us to live. We can discern the truth when we let the Spirit direct our minds and our hearts. Jesus did not leave us as orphans. He gave us His Spirit to be present in us all the time. *"I will not leave you as orphans; I will come to you,"* John 14:18.

Dear Lord,

As I pray today, I thank You for leaving me with the presence of the Holy Spirit who is alive and active within me! Oh, how this treasure of truth brings me great joy! I know I will see You someday face to face! And until then, I have unwrapped Your joyful gift of the Holy Spirit who lives inside me!

In Jesus' Name, Amen

December 13

Are You Hoping While You Wait?

Waiting for answers is hard. We all like to receive answers to our prayers as soon as they are prayed. But as we wait upon the Lord, we develop integrity of heart and uprightness of character. The more we trust our Lord to protect us and guide us, the more He preserves us and promises to give us hope. Our persistent prayers help us grow closer to the Lord as our relationship with Him deepens. We depend more on the Lord when we wait with patience for His will to be done in His timing and for His glory! There is hope in the waiting! *"But if we hope for what we do not see, we wait for it with patience,"* Romans 8:25.

Dear Lord,

I am praising You for Your answers to prayers. Some I have not even seen yet. The answer could be yes, no, or not now, because only You know the rest of the story. You know how it will all work out, so I will praise You while I wait.

In Jesus' Name, Amen

December 14

Do You Want Amazing Grace?

Are you seeking to find forgiveness and wholeness? We are all sinners and need rescuing from our sins. Without help, we will fall. *"For all have sinned and fall short of the glory of God,"* Romans 3:23. We live in a world where we are greatly tempted each day. Without the grace of our Lord, we would never be able to be free from sin. The chains of sin and shame break away when we turn our faces to the Lord and our backs to sin. Only Jesus can give us this amazing grace that flows freely from His open heart. The bad news is that we have all fallen short of the glory of God. But the good news is that we all have been forgiven through the blood of Jesus Christ who paid the price for all our sins! Cling to this good news!

Dear Lord,

I know I am forgiven and free, even a sinner like me! You have taken all my sins and rescued me from guilt and shame. I feel Your amazing grace covering every part of me. I am set free!

In Jesus' Name, Amen

December 15

Is It Possible to Live Peacefully?

Is it possible to love neighbors you disagree with or forgive those who have hurt you? We live in harmony where there is unity. A community divided will fall, but a community united will stand tall. Together, we can strive for peace as we forgive and put aside our differences and offenses to work together for the common good. We all want to live in a place where love reigns because we all have the need to be loved. God created us with this human need. Love mends broken hearts and broken relationships. It starts with a heart filled with love. As we come together and put forth effort to work for unity, our hearts will come together, and the goodness of the Lord will shine forth over all! *"If possible, so far as it depends on you, live peaceably with all,"* Romans 12:18.

Dear Lord,

I will strive to live with Your peace as I work with others who might disagree with me. We all need more harmony and peace in this world where division exists. As I seek more of You, there I will find the peace needed to live peacefully with all.

In Jesus' Name, Amen

December 16

Are You Choosing God's Way?

There are multiple paths we can take and choices we have to make each day. We can go alone or ask for help before we act. God wants us to ask him for direction so He can teach us the right way. We have been taught the rules to follow, but we have free will to choose our way. God hopes we will choose His way! When we act according to the will of God, He is well pleased, and we are at peace in His arms of grace! Choose God!

Dear Lord,

I will keep choosing Your way by seeking Your direction. As I run my race, I will run with Your endurance. I know You have given me others to encourage me as I run. There are clouds of witnesses cheering me on to victory when I choose Your way, the way that leads to life! *"Therefore, since we are surrounded by so great a cloud of witnesses, let us also lay aside every weight, and sin which clings so closely, and let us run with endurance the race that is set before us,"* Hebrews 12:1.

In Jesus' Name, Amen

December 17

Have You Received the
Free Gift from God?

You have been given a gift from God that you must unwrap to receive. When you invite Jesus into your heart and life, you will receive the gift of salvation bought for you by His blood shed on the cross. Jesus has been waiting for you to believe so you can spend eternity with Him and your loved ones who are with Him today. He sees inside your heart and feels your daily struggles with sin. As you let Him in your heart to live, He will set you free from sin and give you another gift, the Holy Spirit, who is real and alive inside of you. If you want these gifts, unwrap and receive them by opening your heart and soul to the Lord and asking for the presence of the Holy Spirit to overshadow you!

Dear Lord,

I have received my gift of salvation from You because I have believed and have been set free from sin. *"For the wages of sin is death, but the free gift of God is eternal life in Christ Jesus our Lord,"* Romans 6:23.

In Jesus' Name, Amen

December 18

Do You See God's Marvelous Light?

We live in times where darkness prevails. There are people hurting all around us. They need God's light. In God, there is no darkness at all. His light overcomes *all* darkness! Have you looked to God to be filled with His light? He will radiate hope within you as you step out of the darkness and into His marvelous light! Come closer to His love and let the light shine in you. Bring His light with you wherever you go. There is someone close to you who needs the light of Christ. Let it shine! *"God is light, and in him is no darkness at all,"* 1 John 1:5.

Dear Lord,

I will keep close to Your light. I know in You there is no darkness at all. This gives me so much hope as I face each day! I am trusting You more each day as I see Your light shining hope in the darkness. I will cling to You, my light and my salvation, and will let Your light shine brightly in me!

In Jesus' Name, Amen

December 19

Are You in God's Waiting Room?

Are you waiting for God to reveal His plan for you? Have you trusted the Lord to speak His wisdom to you? While you are waiting, have you praised Him? While you find yourself in God's waiting room, delight in Him and trust Him. As you trust the Lord with all your heart, He will speak truth to you. He promises to act on your behalf if you commit your way to Him. He will reveal His perfect plan in His time. The more you turn to God, His desires for you will become yours! Delight in the Lord so you will know the desires He puts in your heart! *"Delight yourself in the LORD, and he will give you the desires of your heart,"* Psalm 37:4.

Dear Lord,

I will delight in You as I wait for answers to my prayers! You are working in me while I wait patiently for You. Your goodness shines upon me in the waiting. You tell me, "Trust me more so I can work it all out for you!" I will do that more and more, my Lord!

In Jesus' Name, Amen

December 20

Do You Need Endurance?

We can grow tired and weary of doing good and working hard. We can never please everyone and will not always win. When the going gets tough, it is harder to keep going. As we run our race, we will face struggles along the way and the temptation to quit can grow stronger. But our Lord will never quit on us! He is always with us, in the waiting and the working. He wants us to wait patiently upon Him so He can exalt us at the proper time. He hears our cries for help and will give us endurance to finish our race strong as we press on with Him! Press on to the prize of Jesus Christ, the Author of Life! *"Looking to Jesus, the founder and perfecter of our faith, who for the joy that was set before him endured the cross, despising the shame, and is seated at the right hand of the throne of God,"* Hebrews 12:2.

Dear Lord,

Thank You for helping me push through the pain. You suffered so much for me and yet pressed on. I will keep my eyes on You and keep going with Your strength and endurance!

In Jesus' Name, Amen

December 21

Is Hope Entering the
Inner Place of Your Soul?

We have all experienced suffering in this life. We will continue to struggle and suffer when we make unwise choices. And we suffer when things that are not our fault happen to us in this sinful world where we live. Even people will hurt us and cause us to suffer. But take heart knowing that God will take that suffering and turn it into hope. Yes, when we struggle, there is still hope. Our hope can be found in the living God who makes all things new! He will transform our hearts and renew our minds when we turn towards Him, our anchor of hope! *"We have this as a sure and steadfast anchor of the soul, a hope that enters into the inner place behind the curtain,"* Hebrews 6:19.

Dear Lord,

I can rejoice in this struggle only because my faith is alive and You have given me greater hope that has entered the inner place of my soul! I will set my hope on my living God who has come to bring me back to life!

In Jesus' Name, Amen

December 22

Are You Giving Thanks?

Things will work out for good for those who love God and are called according to his purpose. We all have been invited and called by God. When we accept His calling and act according to His purpose, He will show us His goodness and glory! It is good when we grow in love and live with His grace and kindness. God loves our grateful hearts and wants us to celebrate His goodness in our lives. Let us give thanks with a heart filled with praise and thanksgiving for the many blessings we have received from God whom all blessings flow! *"Oh, give thanks to the LORD, for he is good; for his steadfast love endures forever!"* 1 Chronicles 16:34.

Dear Lord,

Oh, how I love You! I hear You speaking life into me as You place Your steadfast love into my heart. I am basking in the goodness of all You have given me. I cannot thank You enough for Your mercy and love that has changed me!

In Jesus' Name, Amen

December 23

Are You Tuned into Jesus' Channel of Love?

Is your heart heavy because you see others conforming to this world where lies seem to reign over truth? Each one of us faces choices every day about how we will live and who we will follow. We can choose to let our flesh control our thoughts and actions or allow the Spirit of God to lead us. Sin separates us from the love of God when we live selfishly. But there is a way out of sin and a path that leads to life which is found through Jesus Christ! To walk down this narrow road, we must first let our lips and our hearts tune into the love of Jesus. Take refuge in His love under the shadow of His wings and stay tuned into Him. *"How precious is your steadfast love, O God! The children of mankind take refuge in the shadow of your wings,"* Psalm 36:7.

Dear Lord,

I hear You calling me to stay close to You. I will only listen to Your voice as You whisper Your love into my heart, "Come closer to me, my beloved, and listen to my love for you."

In Jesus' Name, Amen

December 24

Are You Resting in His Gentle Arms?

We can find peace when we pursue it. Peace is possible when we open our hearts to the love of Jesus Christ. He is our peace in a world with so much heartache. When our hearts are heavy, His peace will comfort us and give us strength as we draw to Him. When we receive His peace, we can rest in His gentle arms of refuge. Finding eternal peace in a divided world is only possible through Jesus Christ. Perfect peace that passes human understanding will fill our hearts and minds when we turn to Jesus, our Prince of Peace! As you pursue the peace of Christ, others around you will experience peace as well. *"And the peace of God, which surpasses all understanding, will guard your hearts and your minds in Christ Jesus,"* Philippians 4:7.

Dear Lord,

As I speak Your name, I feel peace. As I listen to Your voice, there is a calmness in my soul. "Peace to you, my child," resonates in my mind and my heart and soothes my soul. The gentle whisper of Your voice comforts me and I know I am not alone!

In Jesus' Name, Amen

December 25

Does the Joy of the Lord Reign In You?

There is good news of great joy for us despite the stress around us today. Joy is still possible even when we feel overwhelmed by life's issues. The stress and demands of the world are real and can weigh us down. We can choose to let our hearts be saddened, or we can let the joy of the Lord reign in us. Which are you doing? You will find pure joy lifts you up when your joy is found in Jesus Christ! Because He lives, you can face tomorrow with a smile on your face and eternal joy in your heart. The good news of great joy is for you as you put your trust and faith in Jesus Christ, the Savior of the world, who was born for you. *"For us a child is born, to us a son is given; and the government shall be upon his shoulder, and his name shall be called Wonderful Counselor, Mighty God, Everlasting Father, Prince of Peace,"* Isaiah 9:6.

Dear Lord,

I hear the sweet sound of Your voice telling me, "Dear child, let joy reign in you as you know how much I love you!" As I pray, I will surrender all my stress and let Your great joy come alive in me!

In Jesus' Name, Amen

December 26

Whom Have You Encouraged?

We live in a world where discouragement is more prevalent than encouragement. One criticism after another is spoken from the lips of people, even those we love. We are challenged to stay encouraged as these critical words cut to our hearts. How can we stay encouraged? Jesus wants us to remember He loves us with an everlasting love no matter what we have done. He has forgiven us! Who can we encourage with our love? Jesus wants us to love and encourage others with our gracious words and acts of kindness. Look around you and find someone who needs to know they are loved. Your example of love will bring Jesus to their life in the most wonderful way! *"Therefore encourage one another and build one another up, just as you are doing,"* 1Thessalonians 5:11.

Dear Lord,

You have encouraged me to love as You have loved me. I hear Your words, "Go love that person and encourage that one to press on. Be a light so that others will know my love through your actions of love." I will do as You ask, my Lord.

In Jesus' Name, Amen

December 27

Are You Standing Firm?

Do you have a decision you must make that is weighing you down? Are you struggling with temptations that do not please the Lord? First, turn away from the temptation to sin and turn towards the Lord with all your heart. Worship Him in Spirit and Truth and He will show you the way to go. In Luke 4:8, His Word is clear, *"You shall worship the Lord your God, and him only shall you serve."* As you worship and serve the Lord, He will be your strength and give you the courage to stand up for what is right. Stand up for Christ even when others are sitting down or walking away. Jesus stood up for you, so stand tall with the Lord and you will not fall!

Dear Lord,

I know I must stand firm so I can make the decision that pleases You. As I pray, I am reminded of the way You used the Word of God as Your weapon to fight when You were tempted in the wilderness. I can hear You say, "It is written," to remind me to stand firm in the Word of God.

In Jesus' Name, Amen

December 28

Do You Believe Jesus Will Heal You?

Do you need to be healed? Have you been struggling physically, emotionally, mentally, or spiritually? Do you believe your healing is possible? Turn to the Lord and receive His healing power. He has the power to heal you. As you continue to pray for healing and let Jesus have control, you will find the Lord will heal the places inside of you that need healing. He knows where and how you are struggling. He wants to give you peace deep in your soul. His healing power is present today just as it was years ago. In Luke 5:17, Jesus healed, and it was said, *"And the power of the Lord was with him to heal."*

Dear Lord,

Thank You for healing me. I feel Your power healing all of me. I hear Your comforting voice speaking healing over me as You say, "Heal this child of Mine who believes in My power to heal. Take away her pain and pour comfort over her soul." I am healed in Your mighty presence and power for Your glory!

In Jesus' Name, Amen

December 29

Do You Believe Prayer Changes Things?

You have been given the power and privilege to pray to your Heavenly Father. This power is available communication with your Father through His Son Jesus. Practice prayer and make it a part of your daily life to see a changed heart and relationship that develops. Prayer is a way for you to know you are loved as you bring your requests to a sovereign God who responds to you. Prayer changes things! Do you believe this? Each time you pray, your prayers are beautiful music to God's ears! He bends down to listen to each one lifted to Him! *"I love the Lord, because he has heard my voice and my pleas for mercy. Because he inclined his ear to me, therefore I will call on him as long as I live,"* Psalm 116:1-2.

Dear Lord,

I will keep praying to You because I know You hear my voice and I hear Yours. I hear You telling me, "I am listening to your cries and your praises, I know your heart, and I am here for you, dear child." I will keep lifting my prayers to You!

In Jesus' Name, Amen

December 30

Can You Hear the Voice of Truth?

Are you tired of hearing all the voices arguing about what is correct? Are the opinions of others pulling you away from the truth? Are you listening to the voice of God directing you to all truth? God has so much to tell you because He loves you! He sees your heart and wants what is best for you. His voice of truth will guide and direct you into all truth when you listen and obey Him. His voice is the one you need to listen to so you can know His plan and purpose for you. He will lead you in the right direction and give you all the strength and courage you need! Hear His voice calling you! *"Speak, for your servant hears,"* 1 Samuel 3:10.

Dear Lord,

I just want to hear Your voice, Lord, as I tune out the other voices. As You speak, I hear truth and justice that allows me to step into a new day away from my past that has been pulling me down. With a fresh perspective, I will see You turn the tide towards truth!

In Jesus' Name, Amen

December 31

Do Your Eyes See God's Love?

Are your eyes open to see God's miracles all around you? Have you noticed the love of Jesus present in the eyes of those you love? Are your eyes full of grace? Open your eyes to see God at work around you. Give Him your heart so He can do His miracles in you. Your vision is a gift God has given you so you can see Him in all you do! There are people who need you to be their eyes to see God. Let God show you where to look as you pray. He will open the door to His blessings for you just as He did in Luke 10:23, *"Blessed are the eyes that see what you see!"* Open your eyes and see the blessings of God that await you!

Dear Lord,

I pray to see the many miracles around me. As I gaze at Your beautiful creations, I will see the blessings around me. I hear the sweet melody of Your love as You tell me, "Keep your eyes open to see what I will show you." My eyes are wide open to You always and forever!

In Jesus' Name, Amen

Monthly Reflections

As you pray and lean on the Lord's promises, write what the Lord has revealed to you for this month.

Looking for More?

God-Size Your Prayers to Find Your Destiny

Available on Amazon
https://www.amazon.com/dp/B07TW7YMHV

Also By Jill Lowry

A Year of Daily Devotionals to
Ignite Your Heart for Jesus

Available on Amazon
https://www.amazon.com/dp/B07HKK2MN9